THOUGHTS OF SORTS

GEORGES PEREC

THOUGHTS
OF SORTS

Translated and with an introduction
by David Bellos

A Verba Mundi Book
David R. Godine · Publisher · Boston

This is a *Verba Mundi* Book
published in 2009 by
DAVID R. GODINE, *Publisher*
Post Office Box 450
Jaffrey, New Hampshire 03452
www.godine.com

Copyright © Editions du Seuil, 2003
Collection *La Librairie du XXIe siècle* sous la direction de Maurice Olender.
La première édition de ce recueil posthume a été publiée par Hachette en 1985.

Cet ouvrage, publié dans le cadre d'un programme d'aide à la publication,
bénéficie du soutien du Ministère des Affaires étrangères et du
Service Culturel de l'Ambassade de France aux Etats-Unis.

This work, published as part of a program of aid for publication,
received support from the French Ministry of Foreign Affairs and the
Cultural Services of the French Embassy in the United States.

Translation copyright © 2009 by David Bellos

LIBRARY OF CONGRESS CATALOGING-IN-PUBLICATION DATA
Perec, Georges, 1936–1982.
[Penser, classer. English]
Thoughts of sorts / by Georges Perec ;
translated and with an introduction by David Bellos.
p. cm. — (Verba Mundi ; 13)
Includes bibliographical references.
ISBN 978-1-56792-362-9
I. Bellos, David. II. Title.
PQ2676.E67P4613 2009
844'.914—dc22   2008024870

FIRST PRINTING
Printed in the United States of America

CONTENTS

INTRODUCTION

David Bellos

THOUGHTS OF SORTS gathers a baker's dozen of Georges Perec's essays and occasional pieces written in the last seven years of his sadly short life, which ended in 1982. It was the first collection of his writings to be published posthumously; the selection was made mainly by his fellow-Oulipian, Marcel Bénabou. Its aim was to rescue these varied pieces from the mostly small-circulation periodicals in which they were first published, and also to give a more rounded portrait of Perec's quirky, unorthodox intelligence than was available from his major book-length works. The collection covers the main kinds of writing that interested and attracted Perec outside of his major fiction between the writing of *W, or The Memory of Childhood* (1975) and the (unfinished) composition of his "literary thriller", "*53 Days*", published posthumously in 1989. But, as Perec says in the first of these pieces, his real ambition was "to run through the whole gamut of the literature of my age without ever feeling I was going back on myself or treading ground I had trod before, and to write every kind of thing that it is possible for a man to write nowadays." Alongside these essays, in the years that saw the composition, publication, launch, and afterlife of his masterwork, *Life A User's Manual* (1978), Perec also wrote and translated poetry, composed crossword puzzles and brain teasers, doctored and wrote film scripts, invented now-classic pastiches of literary and scientific language, published travel essays and book reviews, and devised the most haunting (and now most imitated) French short story of his era, "The Winter Journey".

"Statement of Intent" was written for the mass-circulation daily, *Le Figaro*, shortly after Perec won the Prix Médicis for *Life A User's Manual*. Perec was asked to give the broad public a literary self-portrait – in less than eight hundred words. The constraint of length produced a memorable and important piece, which has been much quoted by Perec's critics and admirers. While the agricultural image that he uses to explain the diversity of his work is slightly tongue-in-cheek – Perec's familiarity with farming life was close to zero! – three of the fields that he says he tills (sociology, autobiography, and wordplay) are all well represented in the following twelve chapters. The fourth – long narrative – is obviously absent from this collection of short pieces.

Perec's early profile as a "sociological" writer, earned primarily from *Things* (1965), is underscored here by his essay on reading, which, far from being a piece of literary speculation, seeks to analyze the practical, physical ways in which reading happens in contemporary society. This piece is more a sketch of an idea than a completed research report, but it opens up intriguing vistas that few writers have chosen to follow since then. A related but far less serious essay in social analysis is Perec's digressive musing, "On Spectacles", which, as he says, he never wore, as he enjoyed perfect eyesight throughout his life. This essay was a commission hastily accepted and even more hastily completed with the somewhat intoxicated assistance of his short-sighted friend Julien Etcheverry. It provides an entertaining example of Perec's improvisational wit.

"Three Bedrooms Remembered" is the only extant fragment of an alternative autobiography that Perec imagined in oblique homage to Marcel Proust, whose *Remembrance of Time Past* begins with a description of falling asleep. Perec's project was to tell the story of his life by describing not his waking moments, but where he had slept. The three trial sections that survive relate to his teenage years, at his adoptive parents' weekend house in the country (Blévy), at a house at Nivillers belonging to relatives of his cousin Bianca Lamblin, and at a sanatorium in the town of Enghien-les-Bains. (Olivier Rolin's *Hotel Crystal* is explicitly indebted to Perec's projected "nocturnal autobiography".)

Just as autobiographical and just as oblique is the account Perec gives in "Backtracking" of his analysis with Jean-Bertrand Pontalis between 1971 and 1974. Perec wrote the essay partly in response to Pontalis' transparent use of Perec's case in an essay of his own, which is said to have made Perec angry.* Whatever the prompting, this modest, reflective unraveling, not of the meaning of analysis but of its protocols and framework, ends up subjecting the reader to something that seems to come close to an experience of

---

* Jean-Bertrand Pontalis, "A Partir du contre-transfert: le mort et le vif entrelacés," *Nouvelle Revue de Psychanalyse* 12 (1975), in particular, 81–82. See also David Bellos, *Georges Perec: A Life in Words* (Boston: David R. Godine, Publisher, 1993) 476–77.

analysis itself. But like Perec's writing overall, "Backtracking" leaves the question of whether psychoanalysis really helps open to quite different answers.

"I detest what's called psychology.... I prefer books in which characters are described by their actions, their gestures, and their surroundings...," Perec once said to an interviewer;* and in his "Notes on the Objects to be Found on my Desk" he applies this preference to himself in a whimsical self-portrait of the writer as revealed through the clutter on his writing desk. The product of such writing activity – an unending flow of books – creates the problem dealt with in the fifth piece in this collection, which is also obliquely autobiographical. The friend who tried to stop his book collection at 361 books is none other than Jacques Roubaud, poet, mathematician, Oulipian, and novelist; and it is to Roubaud also that Perec owes his knowledge of the Japanese game of go, played on a board of 19 × 19 (= 361) intersections.**

The third of Perec's self-designated fields of activity – the field of wordplay, rules, and puzzles – can be seen most clearly in his mock-cookery exercise, "81 Easy-Cook Recipes for Beginners". Each recipe consists of four elements (ingredients, first procedure, second procedure, accompaniment). Perec grants himself three alternatives for each of the elements and proceeds to permute all their possible combinations to produce 3^4 ($3 \times 3 \times 3 \times 3 = 81$) different recipes. Easy cooking indeed! Patient readers may

* Interview with Ewa Pawlikowska, *Literature na świece* (Warsaw, 1982) 337‑355.

** Georges Perec, Pierre Lusson, Jacques Roubaud, *Petit Traité invitant à la découverte de l'art subtil du go* (Paris: Bourgois, 1969).

discover that here, too, as in the ground-plan of *Life A User's Manual*, the regulation of the text is broken on purpose, but only once. The intentional bending of the rule, called a *clinamen*, serves to bring the haphazard quality of life itself into an otherwise purely schematic text.

"Twelve Sidelong Glances" and "I Remember Malet & Isaac" relate to lesser-known aspects of Perec's mind that are not captured by the four-field crop rotation model set up in "Statement of Intent". In a distant reflection of Roland Barthes' demythologization of contemporary fashions and advertising techniques (*Mythologies*, 1957), Perec briefly became a cultural critic for a weekly magazine, *Arts-Loisirs*, from October 1966 to March 1967, and in his column he sought to unravel the political and ideological import of current trends. Ten years later, Perec returned to the topics of fashion and advertising, which he mistrusted profoundly, in a piece that is also an exercise in collage. Similarly, his collage of schoolbook typography was intended to lay bare and thus to undermine the ideological agendas implicit in the way history continued to be taught in French schools.

The final essay in this collection, which also gives the volume its title, is the last piece of his own writing that Perec saw in print before he died. It brings together a range of Perec's special contributions to modern literature: his use of the fragment as a literary form; his pursuit of exhaustiveness, combined with his often cunning demonstrations that nothing is ever complete; his fascination with hierarchies, orders, and indexing devices; and his passion for the heteroclite. Is thinking only a matter of putting ideas in a certain order? Or do you have to order your ideas before you can call them thoughts? What are the relations between *sorts* and *thoughts*? Perec's last reflection on the writer's task – which is, in a sense, only to put words in order – is a snapshot of his mind at the time of his death, and a characteristically quizzical summing-up of his entire career.

Throughout these quirky, humorous, personal, and observational pieces runs a thread of sadness that is integral to Perec's project as a writer. What appear to be the two slightest exercises in the collection, "Some Uses of the Verb 'To Live'" and "On the Difficulty of Imagining the Good Life" – one regulated by a dictionary, the other by the alphabet – transmit, by means that are as economical as can be imagined, an awareness of the fragility of living itself and of the shortcomings of each of the twenty-six lives to which we may aspire.

Princeton, New Jersey
16 August 2008

THOUGHTS OF SORTS

STATEMENT OF INTENT

WHEN I ATTEMPT to state what I have tried to do as a writer since I began, what occurs to me first of all is that I have never written two books of the same kind, or ever wanted to reuse a formula, or a system, or an approach already developed in some earlier work.

This systematic versatility has baffled more than one critic seeking to put his finger on the "characteristics" of my writing, and in all probability it has also disheartened some of my readers. It has earned me the reputation of being some sort of computer or machine for producing texts. As I see it, I should rather compare myself to a farmer with many fields: in one field he grows beets, in another wheat, in a third alfalfa, and so on. In like manner, the books I have written belong to four different fields, four different modes of questioning, which, in the last analysis, perhaps address the same problem, but approach it from different perspectives, each of which corresponds, for me, to a specific kind of literary work.

The first of these modes could be called sociological: it has to do with looking at the ordinary and the everyday. It is this mode of questioning which underlies texts like

Things, Species of Spaces, Tentative de description de quelques lieux parisiens, and the work done by the team at *Cause Commune* under the direction of Jean Duvignaud and Paul Virilio. The second mode is of an autobiographical kind: *W, or The Memory of Childhood, La Boutique obscure, Je me souviens, Lieux où j'ai dormi,* etc. The third is the ludic mode, which relates to my liking for constraints, exploits and "exercises", and gives rise to all the work based on the notions and devices gleaned from the Oulipo's experiments: palindromes, lipograms, pangrams, anagrams, isograms, acrostics, crosswords, and so on. The fourth and last is the novelistic mode, and it grows from my love of stories and adventures, from my wish to write books to be read at a gallop: *Life A User's Manual* is the obvious example.

This is a rather arbitrary distribution, and it could be greatly refined. Almost none of my books is entirely devoid of autobiographical traces (for example, an allusion to one of the day's events in a chapter in progress); likewise, almost none is assembled without recourse to one or another Oulipian structure or constraint, even if only symbolically, without the relevant constraint or structure constraining me in the least.

Actually, beyond these four horizons which define the compass of my work – the world around me, my own history, language, and fiction – I think my ambition as a writer would be to run through the whole gamut of the literature of my age without ever feeling I was going back on myself or treading ground I had trod before, and to write every kind of thing that it is possible for a man to write nowadays: big books and small ones, novels and poems, plays, libretti, crime fiction, adventure stories, science fiction, serials and children's books. . . .

I have never felt at ease in talking about my work in theoretical or abstract terms. Even if what I produce seems to stem from a long-worked-out programme, from a long-standing plan, I believe far more that I find my direction by following my nose. From the books I have written, in the order I have written them, I get the sometimes reassuring and sometimes uneasy feeling (uneasy because it is always suspended on a "projected" work, on an incompletion pointing to the unsayable, the desperate object of writing's desire) that they map a path, mark out a space, signpost a fumbling route, describe the specific staging posts of a search which has no *why* but only a *how*: I feel confusedly that the books I have written are inscribed and find their meaning in the overall image that I have of literature, but it seems to me that I shall never quite grasp that image entirely, that it belongs for me to a region beyond writing, to the question of "why I write", which I can never answer except by writing, and thus deferring forever the very moment when, by ceasing to write, that image would visibly cohere, like a jigsaw puzzle inexorably brought to its completion.

1978

Some Uses of the Verb "To Live"

IF I PASS by the building where I reside I can say *I live there*, or, to be more precise, *I live on the first floor at the back of the courtyard*; if I wish to give this assertion a more practical form, I can say *I live at the back of the courtyard, staircase C, middle door*.

If I am standing on my street, I can say *I live over there, at no. 13*, or *I live at no. 13*, or *I live at the other end of the street* or *I live next to the pizzeria*.

If someone in Paris asks where my perch is, I can choose from a dozen or more replies. I could only say *I live in Rue Linné* to someone I knew to be familiar with Rue Linné; most often I would be inclined to specify the geographical location of that street. For instance, *I live in Rue Linné, next to the Saint-Hilaire Hospital* (well-known to taxi drivers), or *I live in Rue Linné, at Jussieu*, or *I live in Rue Linné, near the Zoological Garden*, or *I live in Rue Linné, not far from the mosque*. In more exceptional circumstances I might even say *I live in the Fifth arrondissement*, or *I live in the Latin Quarter*, or for that matter *I live on the Left Bank*.

Anywhere in France (with the specific exception of Paris

and its inner suburbs) I think I can be pretty much certain of making myself understood if I say *I live in Paris*, or alternatively *I live in the capital* (though I don't think I ever have said that), and nothing prevents me from imagining that I might say *I live in the City of Light*, or *I live in the city once called Lutetia*, although that sounds more like the first sentence of a novel than a way of giving an address. On the other hand, I run a serious risk of not being understood if *I say things like I live at latitude 48°50' north by longitude 2°20' east* or *I live 890 kilometres from Berlin, 2,600 kilometres from Istanbul and 1,444 kilometres from Madrid.*

If I lived in Valbonne I could say *I live on the Riviera* or *I live near Antibes.* But as I live in Central Paris, I cannot say *I live in the Paris region* nor *I live in the Paris Basin* nor even *I live in the Department of Seine.*

Nor do I see in which circumstances it might be relevant to say *I live north of the Loire.*

I live in France. I could give this information at any spot located outside of metropolitan France even if I am, officially, in France (for example, in one of the overseas departments); it could only be a witticism to say *I live in the Hexagon*; on the other hand, if I were a Corsican living in Nice, or a native of the Ile de Ré living at La Rochelle, I could perfectly well say *I live on the continent.*

I live in Europe. This type of information could be of interest to an American I might meet, let us say, at the Japanese Embassy in Canberra. "Oh, you live in Europe?" he might say back to me in English, and I would no doubt feel obliged to confess "I am here only for a few (hours/days/weeks/ months)".

I live on Planet Earth. Will I ever have the opportunity of saying that to someone? If it's an extraterrestrial who has dropped in on our world, he would know it already. And if it were to be me, somewhere out towards Arcturus or KX18098B[1], I would certainly have to specify that *I live in the third (and moreover the only inhabited) major planet of the solar system in the order of increasing distance from the sun* or *I live on one of the planets of one of the youngest yellow dwarf stars situated on the fringes of a minor galaxy arbitrarily designated as the Milky Way.* And there would be about one chance in one hundred thousand million billion (that is to say, only 10^{20}) that he would answer: "Oh yes, you mean Earth..."

1981

NOTES ON THE OBJECTS
TO BE FOUND ON MY DESK

THERE ARE many objects on the table at which I work. The oldest is probably my pen; the newest is a small circular ashtray I bought last week. It is white, earthenware, and decorated with an image of the Beirut War Memorial (a memorial, I presume, to the 1914–18 War, not to the war which keeps on breaking out nowadays).

I spend many hours sitting at my desk every day. Sometimes I would like it to be as clear of objects as possible. But usually I like it to be cluttered, almost to excess. The table-top consists of a sheet of glass 140 centimetres long and 70 centimetres wide lying on metal trestles. It is not completely stable, and it is, in fact, not a bad idea for it to be loaded, or even overloaded, since the weight of objects helps to keep it from wobbling.

I still tidy my desk quite often. Tidying consists of putting all the objects on it somewhere else, and then putting them back, one by one. I wipe the glass top with a cloth (that I sometimes dip in a special liquid), and likewise each object. The problem that then arises is to decide whether this or that object should or should not be on the table (and subsequently to find a place for it, but that is by and large not hard to do).

Such restructurings of my environment almost never happen by chance. They occur most often when I am starting or have just finished a piece of work. They arise in the dead of those nebulous days when I don't really know if I'm going to buckle down or not and fall back on displacement activities, namely cleaning up, tidying away, and sorting things out. At such times I dream of an immaculate, unsullied desk-top, with everything in the right place and nothing unnecessary on it, nothing protruding from it, with all my pencils sharpened (but why do I have more than one pencil? I can see six of them, at a glance!), with all my papers in piles, or, even better, with no papers on it at all, just a notebook open at a fresh page (the myth of managing directors' impeccably uncluttered desks: I once saw one that was a small fortress of steel crammed full of electronic (or allegedly electronic) gadgets which rose up and folded away at the touch of a button on an outsize control panel . . .).

Later on, as my work progresses or stalls, my desk gets cluttered with objects brought there sometimes by chance (secateurs, folding ruler) or by temporary needs (coffee-cup). Some of these things will stay on my table for a few minutes, others for a few days, and yet others, which got there for no obviously necessary reason, will settle there permanently. These are not just objects directly connected to the work of writing (paper, stationery, books); some are related to daily habits (smoking), others to occasional habits (snuff-taking, drawing, sweet-eating, playing patience, solving brain-teasers), or to perhaps superstitious obsessions (updating a push-button calendar), or else to nothing in particular, except perhaps a memory of a tactile or visual pleasure, or just a liking for knick-knacks (boxes, stones, pebbles, bud-vases).

Broadly speaking, I could say that the objects on my desk are there because I want them to be there. This is not connected solely to their function, nor solely to my carelessness. For instance, there is no tube of glue on my table. There is one in the little chest of drawers nearby: that is where I put it away just now after using it. I could have left it on my desk, but I tidied it away almost automatically. (I say "almost" because since I am describing what is on my desk I am paying extra attention to what I'm doing with these things.) There are, then, objects of use in my work that are not, or not always, on my desk (glue, scissors, scotch tape, bottles of ink, stapler), and there are objects of no immediate use (a seal) or of another kind of usefulness (a nail-file) or of no use at all (an ammonite) which are on my desk.

In some sense these objects have been chosen, given preference over other objects. For example, it is obvious that there will always be an ashtray on my table (unless I give up smoking), but it will not always be the same ashtray. Generally speaking, an ashtray lasts quite a long time on my desk, but one day, according to criteria it might perhaps be quite interesting to explore, I will put it somewhere else (next to the table where I use my typewriter, for instance, or next to the plank on which I have put my dictionaries, or on a shelf, or in another room) and another ashtray will take its place (but here is a straight contradiction of what I have just asserted: at this very moment, there are three ashtrays on my desk, that is to say, two too many, which are moreover unused; one is the War Memorial, a very recent acquisition; the other, which has on it a charming depiction of the roofscape of Ingolstadt, has just been mended; the one I am using has a base made of black plastic and a white perforated metal lid. As I look at them, as I describe them, I notice in addition that none of them is among my current favourites: the War Memorial is definitely too small to be anything more than a dinner-table ashtray, Ingolstadt is pretty fragile, and as for the lidded black one, the cigarettes I stub out in it go on smouldering for ages...).

A lamp, a cigarette-case, a bud-vase, a stone for striking matches, a cardboard box containing small filing cards of different colours, a large papier-mâché penholder with sea-shell inlays, a glass pencil-holder, several stones, three turned-wood boxes, an alarm clock, a push-button calendar, a lump of lead, a big cigar-box full of knick-knacks (no cigars), a steel spiral device in which you can put pending mail, a polished stone dagger handle, ledgers, exercise books, loose leaves, various writing instruments and accessories, a big blotting stamp, several books, a glass full of pencils, a little gilded-wood box (nothing seems simpler than making a list, but in fact it's much more complicated than it seems: you always leave something out, you're tempted to write etc., but the whole point of an inventory is not to write etc. Contemporary writers (with a few exceptions, such as Michel Butor) have forgotten the art of enumeration: Rabelais's lists, the Linnaean enumeration of fish in *Twenty Thousand Leagues Under the Sea*, the listing of geographers who explored Australia in *The Children of Captain Grant*...

For some years I have been planning a history of some of the objects on the table at which I work; I wrote the beginning nearly three years ago; on rereading it, I notice that of the seven objects I mentioned, four are still on my table (despite the fact that I have moved house in the meantime); two have been replaced: a blotting stamp, replaced by another blotting stamp (the two are very similar, but the second is bigger), and a battery alarm clock (which as I pointed out usually lived on my bedside table, which is where it is today), replaced by a wind-up alarm clock. The third object has disappeared from my desk: it was a cube of perspex made of eight cubes attached to each other in such a way as to allow a great number of different shapes to be made. It was a present from François le Lionnais; it is now in another room, on a radiator shelf, alongside several other puzzles and brain-teasers (one such is on my desk: a double tangram, that is to say two × seven pieces of flat black and white plastic which can be used to make a virtually infinite number of geometrical shapes).

I didn't always have my own desk, I mean, there wasn't always a specific table for me to work at. I do still work now quite often in cafés; but at home it is only once in a blue moon that I work (write) anywhere else than at my desk (for instance, I don't ever really write in bed), and my desk is never used for anything other than my work (once again, as I write these words down I realize that they are not quite correct: two or three times a year, when I give a party, I clear my desk completely, cover it with a paper tablecloth and – like the plank on which I pile my dictionaries – turn it into a serving table).

Thus some kind of a history of my tastes (of their duration, development, and phases) would be part of the work I am planning. To be more precise, it would be one more attempt at defining my place, a somewhat oblique approach to daily life as I live it in practice, a way of talking about my work, my own history and my preoccupations, an effort to pinpoint something which is a part of my experience of the world not in terms of the reflections it casts in distant places, but at the point where it actually breaks surface.

1976

THREE BEDROOMS
REMEMBERED

I. *Blévy: the small bedroom on the first floor*

IT WAS REALLY a very small room, maybe three metres
long and barely two metres wide. The bed was in one corner, just to the left of the door; I think it was a cast-iron
bedstead. To the left of the head of the bed was a window
which looked out onto the road (the road to Brézolles?) and
the boundary wall of the grounds belonging to the house
opposite, which I never went into.

On the wall opposite the bed there was a mantelpiece
(with a big mirror over it?) and on each side of the fireplace
were cupboards: in the left-hand-side cupboard I put my
things, and in the one on the right-hand side there were
books – holiday reading piled up anyhow. The books were
mostly detective and science-fiction stories, and whole runs
of *Mystery-Magazine, Suspense, Alfred Hitchcock Magazine,
Fiction* and others whose names I have forgotten (*Galaxie?*).

That is where I read virtually all the detective novels I
have ever read, and I still remember those which made the
strongest impression on me, even if (in the case of those

17

which I have reread since then by chance, or after having hunted for them for years) I wonder why: Agatha Christies, of course, and especially the Hercule Poirot stories, but also *Tooth and Nail* by Bill Ballinger, *Noon at Grand Central* (by William Irish), *Maid to Kill* (by Pat McGeer?) and for science fiction *The 9 of Spades* by John Amila, *The Dreaming Jewels* by Theodore Sturgeon, although it's not a science fiction novel at all, *The Ape-man Within* by Sprague de Camp which, on reflection, seems pretty feeble to me, and a collection of short stories called *Steps to Infinity*.

Under the window there was a table and a straw-seated chair: a painful memory of summer holidays spent revising for the September resit of exams I had failed in June; on the wall opposite the window there was a little chest of drawers. I don't recall the rest, neither the lighting (a small turned-wood chandelier?), nor the wallpaper, nor the (two?) prints that probably hung on the walls.

II. *Nivillers*

In the early 1950s I spent a few days at the end of the summer in a country house at Nivillers, near Beauvais. I was about fifteen years of age. It was a very pretty house furnished with great care and taste, and in my memory it seems to me that the sole concern of the adults spending their holidays there was to make sure that I didn't touch anything.

I did not sleep in a bedroom but in a converted part of one of the outhouses of the main buildings, maybe a former barn or bakery, which had been transformed into a "tavern": it was a long, almost narrow, low-ceilinged room, with a slightly sunken floor (you went down three steps on entering), lit by two leaded-light windows, which lent itself very well to such a conversion and not much had been needed – a large fireplace with tall fire-dogs (the kind of fireplace that makes you want to say straight away, even if it is obviously wrong, that you could roast an ox in it), pewter measuring cups on the broad beam which formed the mantelpiece, and a long (refectory) table with two long benches – to produce a truer-than-life reconstruction of those half-lit, glimmering halls in which Athos confides his heartaches to d'Artagnan (*The Three Musketeers* was still fresh in my mind).

The bed – a narrow pallet – clashed somewhat with these surroundings, the other significant details of which I have forgotten.

I remember only one other thing about the house: one day, I opened a china box. It held cigarettes which had no doubt been there for years. The paper had yellowed, they were dried out and shriveled like dead things.

That year was the great cycling year (virtually the only cycling year) of my life. I had a racer with handlebars I had taped up myself, like a real pro, with sticking plaster I'd found somewhere, and I rode back to Paris on it, pretending to be Louison Bobet.

III. *Enghien*

In 1946 or 1947 (at the age of ten or eleven) I went for a two-week cure to the spa at Enghien (at that period I had constant sinusitis). I boarded with a (fat?) lady about whom all I remember is that on the first evening she asked me if I was in the habit of saying my prayers before bed.

The bed was a corner of the room. When I was in bed,

the wall was to my left and the bedroom door was at the foot of the bed. The window was on my right. There was a crucifix above the head of the bed with a sprig of box fixed across it.

On the first night a mosquito bit me on the eyelid and for several days I had a very swollen eye.

I have no memory of the treatment. It's the only time I have ever taken the waters. It seems to me that the cure consisted of drinking glasses of tepid, somewhat rust-coloured water which smelt bad (rotten eggs?), and of being sprayed by a hose. It had almost no effect on my sinusitis, which, up to about my twentieth year, resisted more or less all the treatments to which it was subjected.

1977

BRIEF NOTES ON THE ART AND CRAFT OF SORTING BOOKS

EVERY BOOK COLLECTION* corresponds to two needs that are often also obsessions: the need to hang on to things (books), and the need to keep them in some order.

One day a friend of mine thought of stopping his book collection at 361 works. His idea was as follows: once any number n books reaches, by addition or subtraction, the number $K = 361$, which he considered to be if not the ideal then at least an adequate collection of books, to adopt the rule that no new work X be acquired in a permanent way except after the elimination (by gift, by recycling, by sale or by any other effective means) of one prior work Z, such that the total number K of books remains constant and equal to 361:

$$K + X > 361 > K - Z$$

---

* I use the words "book collection" for any set of books assembled by a non-professional reader for his pleasure and daily use. That definition excludes bibliophiles' collections and book bindings bought by the yard for decoration, as well as most specialist collections (academics' libraries, for example) whose problems resemble those of public libraries.

This attractive plan ran into foreseeable obstacles for which the necessary solutions were invented. The first was to consider that one volume – say, from the Pléiade collection of complete works – counted as one (1) book even if it contained three (3) novels (or collections of poetry, or essays, etc.); and from this it followed that three (3) or four (4) or n (*n*) novels by the same author were (implicitly) equal to one (1) volume by said author as the not-yet-collected but ineluctably collectible fragments of his *Complete Works*. And so the view came about that such and such a recently acquired novel by such and such an English novelist of the second half of the nineteenth century could not in logic count as a new work X, but was work Z belonging to a group in progress, namely the set T of all the said novelist's novels (quite a pile, as it happens!). That didn't alter the original idea one jot: simply, instead of talking of 361 works, it was decided that the sufficient book collection should be composed, ideally, of 361 *authors*, whether they wrote one slim volume or a truckload of books. This amendment proved effective over several years, but it soon became apparent that some works – for instance, courtly romances – had no authors, or had several, and that some authors – the Dadaists, for example – could not be split from each other without automatically losing eighty to ninety percent of what made them interesting: and that was how the idea arose of a book collection restricted to 361 *themes* – it's a vague word, but so are the things it sometimes has to cover – and, up to now, this limitation has been rigorously applied.

So one of the main problems to be met by a man who keeps the books he has read or which he promises himself he will read one day is that of the growth of his book collection. Not everyone has the luck of being Captain Nemo:

> The world ended for me on the day when my *Nautilus* first dived beneath the waves. That day I bought my last volumes, my last pamphlets, my last newspapers, and since then I am inclined to believe that humanity has neither thought nor written anything more.

Captain Nemo's twelve thousand volumes in their standard binding were sorted once and for all, and all the more easily because, we are told, no account needed to be taken of the language they were written in (a detail that has nothing to do with the art of sorting books but which is simply intended to remind us that Captain Nemo speaks all languages without distinction). But for us who deal with a world in which people carry on thinking, writing, and publishing books, the problem of book-collection growth is quickly becoming the only real problem: for it is obvious that it is not very difficult to stack ten or twenty books, let's say even a hundred; but when you begin to have 361, or a thousand, or three thousand, and especially when the total begins to grow almost every day, the problem arises, first, of stacking all those books somewhere, and then of being able to track them down again when, one day, for one reason or another, you want or you need to read or even to reread them.

Thus the book collection problem proves to be a double one: a spatial problem in the first place, and in the second place a problem of order.

1. On Space

1.1 *General Considerations*

Books are not dispersed but gathered together. Just as you put all your jars of jam on the jam-jar shelf, you put all your books in a same place or in several same places. You could stuff all your books in packing cases if all you wanted to do was to hang on to them, or you could pile them up in the cellar or the attic or in the back of your cupboards – but generally speaking, people prefer books to be seen.

In practice, books are most often placed next to each other along a wall or partition on parallel, linear support-ing devices of no more than adequate depth and without excessive intervals between them. Books are – generally speaking – stacked upright and in such a way as to leave vis-ible the lettering printed on their spines (sometimes, as in bookshop window displays, the front jacket is shown, but what is most unusual, in fact ruled out and almost always considered shocking, is a book displaying only its cut edge).

In contemporary interior design, bookcases are corners: "book nooks". Such pieces of furniture usually consist of a module belonging to a living room suite which includes:

    a drop-leaf drinks unit
    a drop-leaf writing-desk unit
    a two-door display cabinet module
    a hi-fi housing unit
    a television module
    a slide-projector unit
    a glass-fronted wall cupboard
    etc.

and they are shown in catalogues with a few dummy bind-ings on them for decoration.

However, in practice, books can be gathered together almost anywhere.

1.2 *Places where books can be put*

in the hall
in the living room
in the bedroom(s)
in the toilet(s)

Generally only one kind of book is ever put in the kitchen, the kind known specifically as "cookery books".

It is extremely unusual to find books in the bathroom despite the fact that for many people the bathroom is a favorite place to read. Ambient damp is universally thought to be the principal threat to the longevity of printed matter. At the most you might find in the bathroom a medicine chest and in the medicine chest a little pamphlet entitled *What to do before the doctor comes*.

1.3 *Places where books can be put* (continued)

On mantelpieces or radiator shelves (however, it should be remembered that heat can turn out to be somewhat harmful in the long term)

between two windows

in the recess formed by a blocked-off doorway

on the steps of a library stool, making the aforementioned unusable (very chic, cf. Ernest Renan)

under a window

on a unit placed sideways to the wall and dividing the room into two (very smart, looks even better with a few house-plants).

1.4 *Things which are not books but which are often encountered in bookcases*

Photographs in gilt-iron frames, small prints, pen-and-ink drawings, dried flowers in stem vases, match-strikers with or without sulphur matches (dangerous), tin soldiers, a photograph of Ernest Renan in his office at the Collège de France, postcards, doll's eyes, boxes, sachets of salt, pepper, and mustard with the compliments of Lufthansa, letter-scales, X-hooks, marbles, pipe-cleaners, scale models of vintage cars, multicoloured pebbles and gravel, ex-votos, springs.

2. On Order

If you do not keep on sorting your books, your books unsort themselves: it is the example I was given to try to get me to understand what entropy was: personal experience has provided me with frequent demonstrations of it.

An unsorted book collection is not a serious matter in itself. It is a problem of the same order as: "Where did I put my sock?" You always believe that you will know intuitively where you have put this or that book; and even if you do not know, you will not have too much trouble going through all your bookshelves to find it.

This apologia of comfortable untidiness contrasts with the pettifogging delights of personal bureaucracy: a thing for every place and every thing in its place, and vice versa. Torn between these two poles, the right to be laid-back, easy-going, and anarchic, and the virtue of the clean slate, the steely efficiency of the great clear-out, you always end up trying to sort out your book collection. It's a nerve-wracking, depressing operation which can nonetheless bring pleasant surprises, such as when you find a book you had forgotten you had from not having seen it for so long, and, putting off to the morrow what can't be done today, you lie flat on you bed and reread it from cover to cover.

2.1 *Ways of sorting books*

in alphabetical order
by binding
by continent or by country
by colour
by date of acquisition
by date of publication
by format
by genre
by literary period
by language
by order of reading
by series

None of these orders is satisfactory in isolation. In practice, every book collection is arranged according to some particular blend of these sorting criteria. The weighting given to each criterion, its resistance to change, its obsolescence and its capacity to survive, are what gives a collection of books its own unique personality.

We should first of all distinguish stable sorting orders from temporary ones. Stable orders are those which you intend in theory to continue to observe; temporary ones are intended to last but a few days: until the book finds or returns to its definitive place – in the case, for instance, of a recently-acquired and still unread book, or a recently-read book which you are not too sure where to put and which you have promised yourself you will put away the next time you have a "big sort", or again it could be a book you have been reading and which you don't want to put away until you have got back to it and finished it, or again it could be a book which you have been using constantly over some period of time, or a book you have got out to look up some reference or piece of information and which you haven't yet put back, or a book you could not possibly put in its right place because it does not belong to you and you have promised many times to return it, and so on.

As far as I'm concerned, about three-quarters of all my books have never been really sorted. Those which are not shelved in a definitively provisional manner have, as in the OuLiPo, provisionally definitive positions. In the meantime, I shift them from room to room, from shelf to shelf, from stack to stack, and I sometimes spend three hours hunting for a book without finding it, but occasionally enjoying the satisfaction of unearthing six or seven others which will do just as well.

2.2 Books which are very easy to sort

Big Jules Verne volumes in red bindings (either the real Hetzel editions or the Hachette reissues), very large books, very small books, Baedekers, rare (or supposedly rare) books, books in special bindings, volumes from the Pléiade collection, from the *Présence du Futur* collection, novels published by Editions de Minuit, book series (*Change, Textes, Les Lettres nouvelles, Le Chemin*, etc.), periodicals of which you have at least three issues, etc.

2.3 Books which are not too hard to sort

Books about cinema – whether they are monographs on directors, star albums, or shooting scripts; Latin-American novels, ethnology, psychoanalysis, cookery books (see above), directories (next to the telephone), German romantics, handbooks in the *Que sais-je?* series (the problem with these being whether to sort them as a single category or to distribute them according the subject they deal with), etc.

2.4 Books which are well-nigh unsortable

All other books, for example: periodicals of which you have only one issue, or Clausewitz's *The Russian Campaign of 1812*, translated from the German by M. Bégouën, 31st Dragoons, Staff College Certificate, with one map, Paris, Chapelot & Co. Military Publishers, 1900, or else fascicle 6 of volume 91 (November 1976) of the *Publications of the Modern Language Association of America* (PMLA) containing the programme of the 666 sessions of the said association's annual congress.

Like the librarians in Borges's Babel looking for the book which holds the key to all the others, we waver between the illusion of completion and the abyss of the ungraspable. In the name of completion we would like to believe that a single order exists which would allow us immediate access to knowledge; in the name of the ungraspable we wish to believe that order and disorder are two identical terms signifying chance.

It is equally possible that they are but two traps, optical illusions designed to mask the attrition of books and systems.

But it is no bad thing, in the meantime, for our book-shelves to find occasional alternative uses as memory-joggers, cat-hammocks and glory-holes.

1978

Twelve Sidelong Glances

1

Off the Peg

JACQUARD POLO-NECK TOP (215 F) over a pure new wool flannel dress (420 F); Liberty-pattern woollen pleated skirt (295 F), open-work top (360 F) over a tartan-background woollen jumper with Jacquard neck-line (185 F).

Pure wool golfing trousers (250 F), Jacquard shawl-collar jacket (225 F) over a matching sweater (165 F); pure wool kilt (230 F), woollen sailor-suit jacket (250 F).

Pure wool wrap-round kilt with flap pockets (235 F); V-neck button-up waistcoat (195 F); pleated tartan flannel skirt (280 F), pure wool Peter Pan jacket (265 F).

Printed muslin dress, silk collar and cuffs, pleated skirt (400 F).

Stone-washed, striped V-neck pullover, synthetic fibre (175 F), matching scarf (65 F) over culottes in acetate multi-fibre (300 F); flowing rayon dress (370 F) under a long geometric-pattern cardigan, synthetic fibre (235 F).

Printed artificial crêpe outfit: straight jacket with pleated collar, pleated skirt (450 F); synthetic muslin outfit, flower printed: pleated skirt, square-collar, V-neck top, flared cuffs (500 F).

Pure jersey wool dress, silk shawl collar and cuffs, ribbed top, flared skirt (450 F); pure jersey wool outfit, silk sailor-suit collar, ribbed sleeves and pockets, pleated skirt, button-on foot-straps (525 F).

Pure wool flannel outfit: tailored collar jacket, short buttoned waistcoat, fully pleated skirt (790 F), round-necked silk blouse with bow (250 F).

Pleated jersey wool cloak with matching skirt and pleated front panel (420 F).

Children's collection: printed satin country pinafore. Four-year-olds: 90 F.

Jacquard pullovers and tops from 115 to 155 F (6 to 8 years) according to style. Coordinated scarves (65 F), berets (55 and 75 F).

On an impressive number of posters displayed on the still-new bus shelters for about a fortnight last October, three kids with devastatingly childlike looks showed off to best advantage the pullovers, berets, and scarves described above: their poses, expressions, dress, and relationship to each other, both at the level of advertising mythology as well as at the level of what one could suppose to be reality (their existences as advertising models, the role they were being made to play, the roles they played to themselves, the pyramid of psychological and financial investments of which they were simultaneously the objects and the means) seemed to me to be one of the most repugnant manifestations of the world in which we live.

2
Leather goods

Fashion could just as well be what sets things apart as what brings them together: communing in a higher value, "we happy few", etc. That could be imagined, after all. But, at the risk of being accused of aristocratism, I continue to wonder why so many people are proud to exhibit handbags bearing their makers' monograms. If you set store by having your own initials on things you are fond of (your shirts, suitcases, napkin rings, etc.), well, why not?; but your supplier's initials? That, I'm afraid, is beyond me.

3
"Les Must"

The key word of fashion is not: "Do you like it?" but "You must".

You must. "It's a must". Which is what a Paris jeweller has called his collection of lighters and watches.

What strikes me is not so much the name itself, but the fact that it is followed by a little R in a circle which means that the manufacturer reserves exclusive rights to the use of this name.

The fashionable object is of little consequence here. What matters is the name, the brand, the signature. One could even say that if the object were not named and signed it would not exist. It is nothing except its own sign. But signs wear out fast, much faster than lighters or watches. Which is why fashion changes.

People say this is but a gentle tyranny. But I'm not so sure.

4

In brackets: an anecdote

Some years ago I had occasion to eat four meals in the space
of three months in four Chinese restaurants located respectively in Paris (France), Saarbrücken (West Germany),
Coventry (England) and New York (USA). The restaurants
had more or less the same décor, using virtually identical
signs (dragons, ideograms, lamps, lacquer-work, red tapes-
try, etc) to signify Sinosity. As for the food, things were much
less obvious: lacking the point of reference, I had thought
naively, up to then, that (French) Chinese cuisine was Chinese cuisine: but (German) Chinese cuisine turned out to
resemble German cuisine, (English) Chinese cuisine was
just like English cuisine (pea-green peas, etc.), (American)
Chinese cuisine was not remotely like anything Chinese
except something typically American.

This anecdote seems to me to be full of meaning, but I
don't know what, exactly.

5

Quotations

Fashion: the changing and whimsical element in social customs, the element reigning over personal decoration, dress,
furnishing, carriages, etc. The word properly means *manner*, i.e. the manner which is by definition the right one and
which needs no justification. However, fashion, transient as
it is, is rooted in the whims of often poor taste and seeks to
flatter the vanity and to vary the pleasures of the high-born,
wealthy and idle; more or less unknown to the lower

classes, fashion nonetheless supports a host of industrious workers. Orientals have passions rather than tastes, wishes rather than caprices: their institutions, ideas and customs have an almost inflexible stability. Fashion, unheard of in the East, is, on the contrary, all-powerful in civilized Europe, especially in France, where rapid and superficial impressions follow one upon the other. (Bachelet and Dezobry, *Dictionnaire général des Lettres, des Beaux-Arts et des Sciences morales et politiques.* Paris, Delagrave, 1882.)

Paris fashions, outstanding particularly for their taste and elegance, are adopted almost universally by foreign nations, and articles of fashion are amongst the main goods exported; the taxes levied by French customs on exports of fashion goods alone exceeds five million francs per annum. (Bouillet, *Dictionnaire universel des Sciences, des Lettres et des Arts*, Paris, Hachette, 1854.)

6

Questions, 1

Why talk of fashion? Is it really an interesting subject?

A fashionable subject?

A broader question could be asked about those modern institutions like fashion, sport, "holidays", social life, educational methods, "nature conservancy", the cultural environment, etc., which, it seems to me, turn into a trial, if not into suffering or even into torture, activities which, to begin with, were only ever intended to be a pleasure or a joy (cf. Georges Sebbag, *Le Masochisme quotidien* [The masochism of everyday life], Paris, Le point d'être, 1972).

A fashionable object is said to be all the rage. But is not

fashion itself a rabid disease, a raging fury? Not just raging, moreover, but also noise, thundering, ear-splitting. Fashion's got no respect for peace and quiet; it's a pain in the drum.

7

On the Other Hand...

It should be a question of enjoyment: of the enjoyment to be had from our bodies, from play, from dressing, from dressing the same way or dressing differently, the enjoyment of discovering or inventing or returning to something, the pleasure of changing.

It would be called fashion: a kind of excitement, the feeling of a celebration, of lavishness; something of no moment, something useless, gratuitous, and pleasant. You would think up a dish, or gesture, a form of words, a game, a piece of clothing, an excursion, a dance, you would share your invention with others and share the inventions of others. It might last a few hours or a few months; you would tire of it, or pretend to; it would be revived, or not, as the case may be. It would be the way it was at school, in the playground; first it was prisoner's base, then tag-ball, then fives, then skiffle-bands of combs and loo-paper, then collecting cigarette packets.

But obviously it's not like that, not like that at all. Even before you begin to talk about fashion, in advance of fashion phenomena being illuminated by the more or less flickering lights of contemporary ideologies, you already know it won't be like that at all.

Yet the language of fashion itself speaks of caprice, spontaneity, fantasy, invention, frivolousness. But it lies. Fashion is entirely on the side of violence – the violence of conformism, of obeisance to models, the violence of the social consensus and its veiled scorn for the excluded.

8
Questions, 2

You can't expect to get a lot out of an attack on fashion. Fashion exists. Everyone knows that. Fashions are made and unmade, produced and distributed, bought and consumed. Fashion enters into most parts of our everyday lives.

All fashion phenomena lead towards a single basic observation: fashion produces neither objects nor events, but only signs: the landmarks which allow a collectivity to cohere. The only question is then this: why do we need these signs? Or, to put it another way, why do we not find these signs somewhere else?

What can be done, when the very existence of fashion looks like a crude and vulgar institution (something like a carrot at the end of a stick) relating to the weary convulsions of our mercantile civilization? Can one evade fashion? Subvert fashion? Or what?

9
Alternatives

Without disputing the existence of fashion or doubting the validity of its principles, various modifications of fashion phenomena can be suggested:

a) variation of periodicity

Fashion is generally seasonal. But it could be made to be monthly, weekly or, best of all, daily. For example, there would be Monday clothes, Tuesday clothes, Wednesday clothes, Thursday clothes, Friday clothes, Saturday clothes and Sunday best. And similarly for all other kinds of fashion.

Being "bang up-to-date" would then at last mean something.

b) multiplication of fields

Many things, places, people, etc. are fashionable. More fashions could be created, in areas where up to now fashion has but rarely strayed. For example, even dates could become fashionable. Or banks. Cafés, restaurants and stores have piled themselves high with oil-lamps and old-fashioned cash registers. Which brave banker will open a branch decked out as a saloon bar (a guaranteed winner)? And who will make the metro station at Corentin-Celton the latest craze? – "Detrain at C. C., the top peoples' stop!"

c) intensification of incoherence

It has been widely noted that fashion is eclectic, that is to say, it includes models, men, and works which might have been thought to be irreconcilable (this is true not only of clothing fashions – skirts of every length are now fashionable – but also of almost all artistic fashions). It would require only a slight intensification of this tendency to create a world in which everything was in fashion.

d) heightened exclusiveness

This would be the opposite direction. There would be, at any given moment in any given field, only one single thing in fashion: for example, tennis shoes, or *chili con carne*, or Bruckner's symphonies. Then it would all change: waders, *tarte tatin*, Corelli's church sonatas. To lend weight to the matter (and to allow the rulers of our land to deal more effectively with the economic problems they have to face), we could grant these exclusive imperatives the force of law: the public would be alerted in good time by announcements in the press of the manner in which they will be required to be shod, fed, and musically entertained.

e) Finally, fashion could be imagined no longer as a temporal phenomenon, but as a function of place. Fashions would no longer be distributed chronologically, but spatially; no longer would fashions be subjected to fluctuating rhythms and imponderable contingencies, no longer condemned inexorably to wasting away at greater or lesser speed, they would no longer live but a day, nor suffer from the mediocrity of their periodic and disenchanted revivals.

All fashions would exist simultaneously and would be distributed about the entire surface of the planet; getting to know them would no longer be a seasonal matter, but a question of distance.

Wherever you went you would never find what you had already seen here. Travelling would then perhaps regain its meaning: you would see new things. In everyone's heart of hearts would lie a dormant Marco Polo, dreaming of visiting the land of fur, the land of the sauerkraut-eaters, or the land of thick woolly jumpers...

10

Or rather

Fashion heightens the instability of things, the ungraspable, oblivion: it trivializes lived experience by reducing it to trivial signs, to the trickery of simulated antique gloss or of simulated leather, to the vulgarity of imitations. The trivialization of an already trivial original, reduced to bare bones with a forged certificate of authenticity: the brand-new quaintly pre-aged, or pseudo-synthetic imitation-style paste diamonds. Even the connivance is artificial, for there is no dialogue: what you share is the poverty of a code without substance: the last word...

The opposite of fashion is obviously not the unfashionable. It can only be the present – what is there, what is rooted, permanent, resistant, lived-in: an object and the memory of it, a being and its history.

It is no great use to be or to want to be against fashion. All that you can want, perhaps, is to be on the side, somewhere where fashion's rule (what's in/what's out) holds no sway.

That could come about by simply paying attention to a piece of clothing, to a colour, to a gesture, or merely by enjoying a taste shared in the secret serenity of a habit, of a history, of an existence.

And so:

11
The Pillow Book

Outerwear
In winter I prefer azalea.
I also like shiny silk, and white robes with dark crimson linings.
In summer I like mauve and white.

Fan handles
With yellow-green paper, I like red handles.
With mauve-purple paper, a green handle.

Women's robes

I like light colours. The colour of vine-leaves, pale green, cherry-leaf hue, plum red, all light colours are pretty.

Chinese jackets

I like red and wisteria. In summer I prefer mauve; in autumn, "dry heather".

Skirts with long trains

I like skirts decorated with sea-coral motifs. Overskirts.

Jackets

In spring I like azalea and cherry-leaf hue. In summer, I like "green and dead leaf" jackets, or "dead leaf".

Materials

Grape-coloured material, and white fabric, and fabrics with serrated oak-leaves embroidered on a soft green background. Red plum fabrics are also pretty but they are so often seen that I am weary of them more than of anything else.

(Adapted from *The Pillow Book of Sei Shônagon*)

12

Or else, finally:

Instead of trying to get to grips with an elusive object, I would rather have begun telling, in the wake of that lady-in-waiting who died around the year 1000, the stories of some of the objects on the desk where I work: a blotter, a carved stone dagger-handle, a Britannia-metal bud-vase, three turned-wood boxes, a block for striking matches shaped like a truncated cone with an orange-coloured base, a thin sandstone slab decorated with a landscape painting, a papier-mâché penholder with sea-shell inlays, a tea-pot shaped like a cat, and a box of 144 "round-hand" Baignol & Farjon ink-pens, etc.

Those stories, no doubt, have been marked by fashion. But they will not have been exhausted by contact with it.

1976

BACKTRACKING

FOR FOUR YEARS, from May 1971 to June 1975, I underwent analysis. Hardly had the analysis finished than I was assailed by the desire to say, or, more exactly, to write down what had taken place. Shortly after, at a meeting of the editors of the review *Cause Commune*, Jean Duvignaud proposed an issue on the theme of "cunning", and I decided there and then that my text would fit most obviously into just such a framework which, for all the difficulty of its precise definition, would encompass matters volatile, vague, and oblique.

Fifteen months have gone by since then, and I have made maybe fifty attempts to get beyond the first lines of a text which, after a few sentences (roughly, those which I have just written), foundered every time on ever more muddled rhetorical devices. I wanted to write, I had to write, I had to restore in and through writing the trace of what had been said (and all those pages begun again, those abandoned drafts, those lines left hanging, are like memories of shapeless sessions where I had the indescribable feeling of being a weightless word-machine), but the writing froze solid in disclaimers and allegedly prior questions: Why do I need to write this text? Who is it really for? Why choose to write and publish, to make public what was perhaps only ever named in the privacy of analysis? Why decide to hang this wavering effort on the two-pronged hook of "cunning"? That made a whole list of questions I asked with suspicious energy – little a, little b, little c, little d – as if there just had to be questions, as if without questions there could be no answers. But what I have to say is not an answer to anything, it is an affirmation, something obvious, something that happened, that arose. Not something that was buried at the heart of some problem, but something that was there, right next to me, something of me to tell.

Cunning gets round things, but how do you get round cunning? It's a trick question, a cover question, a pretext serving, each time, to defer the inevitable commencement of writing. Each word I set down wasn't a milestone but a diversion, the stuff of daydreams. For fifteen months I daydreamed on those meandering loop-words just as, for four years, I had daydreamed on the couch as I gazed at the moulding and plaster-cracks on the ceiling.

Then, as now, it was almost a comfort to tell myself that one day the words would come. One day talking would begin, writing would flow. For years you think that talking means finding, discovering, understanding, understanding at last, being illuminated by truth. But it doesn't. When it comes, all you know is that it has come; it's there, you're talking, you're writing. Talking is only talking, simply talking, writing is just writing, making the shapes of letters on a blank piece of paper.

Did I know that that was what I had sought – that eternally unsaid obviousness forever waiting to be said, that expectation alone, that sole tension recovering an almost intangible mumbling?

It happened one day, and I knew it had happened. I would like to be able to say I knew straightaway, but that would not be true. There is no tense to express when it was. It took place, it had taken place, it takes place, it will take place. You knew it already, you know it now. Just a thing that opens and has opened: your mouth opens to speak, your pen is open for writing: something shifted, something shifts and makes a mark, the wavy line of ink on paper with its up-strokes and down.

I assume from the start that the equivalence of speaking and writing is obvious, just as I assimilate the blank sheet of paper to that other place of hesitations, illusions, and crossings-out, the ceiling of the analyst's consulting room. I know it is not obvious, but it is for me, from now on, and it is exactly that point that was at stake in the analysis. That is what happened, that is what was shaped from session to session over a period of four years.

Psychoanalysis is really not at all like the advertisements for remedies for baldness: these wasn't a "before" and an "after". There was a present of analysis, a "here and now" which began, went on, and drew to an end. I could just as well write "which took four years to begin" or "which went on ending for four years". There was no beginning and no end: long before the first session an analysis had already begun, if only in the slow decision to undertake one and in the choice of an analyst. Long after the last session the analysis continues, if only in this solitary duplication which mimics its persistence and plodding. The tense of analysis was a stuckness in time, a time-balloon: for four years there was an everydayness of analysis, a routine: little marks in a diary, work strung out through the fabric of sessions, their regular recurrence, their rhythm.

In the first place analysis was just that: a particular way of separating days – days on and days off – and on days on, something resembling a fold, a retreat, a warp; in the layering of the hours, a suspended, alien moment; a kind of halt, a pause in the day's flow.

There was something abstract in this arbitrary time, something which was both reassuring and fearful, an immovable and timeless time, a stationary time in an implausible space. Yes, of course, I was in Paris, in a neighbourhood I knew well, in a street I had even lived in once, a few yards from my favourite bar and several familiar restaurants, and I could have played at working out my longitude, latitude, altitude, and orientation (my head was west by north-west, my feet facing east by south-east). But the ritual order of the sessions excerpted them from the space and time of these coordinates: I arrived, I rang, a girl opened the door. I waited a few minutes in a room set aside for this purpose: I could hear the analyst showing the preceding client to the door: a few moments later, the analyst opened the waiting room door. He never crossed the threshold. I passed in front of him and preceded him into the consulting room. He followed me, closed the doors – there were two, which created a tiny entrance hall, something like an airlock emphasizing the enclosure of the space – then went and sat down in his armchair, whilst I stretched out on the couch.

I stress these ordinary details because they were repeated two or three times a week for four years, just as the end-of-session ritual was repeated: the door-bell rung by the following client, the analyst mumbling something like "Good" without the word ever implying any kind of appreciation of the stuff that had been stirred during the session, then, standing up, with me getting up also and, when appropriate, paying him his fee (I didn't pay at every session, but fortnightly), with him opening the doors of his consulting room and showing me to the main door and closing it behind me after a ritual leave-taking which most often consisted of a confirmation of the day of the next session ("Until Monday" or "See you Tuesday", for example).

At the next session, the same movements, the same gestures were repeated exactly, identically. On the few occasions when they were not repeated, and however minute the modification may have been to one of these elements of ritual and even if I do not know which one it was, the variation signified something, perhaps only that I was in analysis, and that analysis was that and not anything other. It is of little matter, as it happens, whether these modifications came from the analyst, from me, or by chance. These tiny gaps, whether they made the analysis spill over into the convention in which it was wrapped (as for example, when on very rare occasions I took the initiative and opened the doors to leave by myself) or, on the contrary, robbed the analysis of a piece of time that belonged to it (such as when, in the absence of his secretary, the analyst answered the telephone himself or had to let in the next client or deal with a Salvation Army collector at the door), all announced the function that these rituals had for me: to put a frame of space and time around that unending discourse of which in the course of sessions, over months and years, I was going to try to take possession and in which I was going to seek to recognize myself and to give myself a name.

The regularity of these entry and exit rituals thus became

47

for me a first rule (not of psychoanalysis in general, but only of the only experience I could have of it and of my memory of that experience): immutable by agreement, repeated calmly, these rituals were a serenely polite way of marking the boundaries of the closed space beyond the city's hubbub, beyond time, out of this world, where something was going to be said which would perhaps come from me, be mine, be for me. The rituals seemed to guarantee the benevolent neutrality of the unmoving ear to which I was going to try to say something, they were, so to speak, the bounds – polite, civilized, slightly austere, slightly cold, a touch stilted – within which the sneaking, stopped-up violence of analysis would burst out.

For four years I came, stretched out on the couch, put my head on a white handkerchief which, before the arrival of the next client, the analyst would throw casually onto the top of a little Empire filing cabinet already strewn with the crumpled antimacassars of preceding clients, cross my hands behind my neck or on my stomach, stretch out my right leg and bend my left leg slightly, and plunge into that time without history, that non-place which was going to become the place of my history, of my speaking still to come. I could see three walls, three or four pieces of furniture, two or three prints, a few books. The floor was carpeted, there were mouldings on the ceiling and hessian on the walls; the room was plain and always tidy, seemingly neutral, changing little from one session to another, from one year to the next. A dead, calm place.

There was not much noise. A piano or a radio, sometimes, usually far off; someone, somewhere using a vacuum cleaner, or, on fine days when the analyst left the window open (he often aired the room between sessions), birdsong from a nearby garden. The telephone, I've already said this, almost never rang. The analyst himself made very little noise. Sometimes I could hear his breathing, or a sigh, or a cough, or stomach rumbles, or the striking of a match. So I had to speak. That's what I was there for. That was the rule of the game. I was shut into this other space with another person: the other was sitting in an armchair behind me, he could see me, he could speak or not speak, and generally chose not to speak; whereas I was stretched out on the couch in front of him. I could not see him. I had to speak, my speech had to fill this empty place.

But speaking was easy anyway. I needed to talk, and I had a storehouse, an arsenal of stories, problems, questions, associations, fantasies, puns, memories, hypotheses, explanations, theories, frames of reference, and ways of hiding.

I skipped along the paths of the maze I had made for myself, following suspiciously legible signposts. It all had meaning, it was all connected, obvious, and could be unravelled at will: signs waltzed by, proffering their charming anxieties. But beneath the ephemeral flashes of verbal collisions and the controlled titillation of the beginner's book of Oedipus, my voice encountered only its own emptiness. It did not engage with the faint echo of my own past or with the clouded turbulence of my affrontable enemies, but came up only with the hackneyed refrains of mummy and daddy, willy and wallop; my real emotions, fears and desires were masked by off-the-shelf answers, by mechanical operators that were not mine, by the thrills of a fairground railway.

Such dizzying bouts of universal meaningfulness prompted whirls of word associations, but they abated quite quickly, in a few seconds, in fact, a few seconds of silence during which I waited for the analyst's acquiescence, which was never given, and I would then fall back into a morose and bitter state, further than ever from my own speech, from my voice.

The other, behind me, said nothing. At every session I waited for him to speak. I was sure he was keeping something from me, something he knew far more about than he was prepared to admit, something that was nonetheless in the mind, that he knew where he was going. As if the words that went through my head flew straight into his head and settled deep inside it, building up over the sessions a neat lump of silence as dense as my speech was hollow, as full as my speech was empty.

From then on mistrust set in and enveloped my words as well as his silence: it became a tiresome game of reflections, images returning their Möbius strips to infinity, dreams too good to have been dreamt. Where was truth? Where was untruth? When I tried to be silent and stop myself from getting stuck in feeble regurgitation or in illusions of the intimation of speech, silence immediately became unbearable. When I tried to speak, to say something of me, to get to grips with the clown inside me who juggled so cleverly with my story and conjured with such brilliance as to mystify himself, I felt immediately as if I was starting again on the same puzzle, as if, by going through all the possible combinations of pieces one by one, I might one day find the image I was after.

At the same time something like a crash in my memory set in. I became afraid of forgetting, as though unless I made a note of everything I would be unable to hold on to any part of passing life. Every evening, scrupulously, with obsessive conscientiousness, I entered up a kind of log. It was the complete opposite of a "personal" diary; I only entered in it "objective" things that had happened to me: time of waking, timetable, journeys, purchases, progress in work (measured in lines or pages), people met or just seen, details of the evening meal I had eaten in this or that restaurant, books read, records listened to, films seen, etc.

As I panicked at the prospect of losing track of myself, I began to collect and to sort things in a frenzy. I kept everything: letters and their envelopes, cinema ticket stubs, bills, cheque stubs, circulars, receipts, catalogues, summonses, weeklies, used felt-tips, empty lighters, and even receipts for gas and electricity payments for a flat I hadn't lived in for more than six years; sometimes I would spend whole days sorting and filing, thinking up a system which would have a place for every year, every month, every day of my life.

I had been doing the same thing with my dreams for some time already. Long before the beginning of my analysis I had begun to wake myself up in the night to write notes on my dreams in black notebooks which never left me. Very soon I became so practiced that dreams offered themselves to me fully written, including their titles. Irrespective of my present feelings about these dry and secret utterances in which my own story seems to me to be reflected only through a thousand refracting prisms, I do now concede that these dreams were not lived to become dreams, but dreamt to become texts, that they were not the "royal road" that I thought they would be, but winding paths taking me ever further away from a proper recognition of myself.

Made cautious perhaps by the cunning of my dreams, I transcribed nothing, or almost nothing, of my analysis. A sign in my diary – the analyst's initials – indicated the date and time of the session. In my log, I just wrote "session" followed sometimes by an adjective, usually pessimistic ("gloomy" "dull", "stringy", "pretty miserable", "boring", "crappy", "bloody stupid", "bloody shitty", "depressing", "useless", "harmless", "wistful", "scrappy and scrappable", etc.).

Very occasionally I marked the session by something the analyst had said that day, by an image or a feeling (for instance, "cramp"), but most of these notations, both positive and negative ones, have now lost their meaning and all the sessions – with the exception of a few, when there rose to the surface the words which would bring the analysis to its term – are now merged together in a memory of waiting, with my eyes stranded on the ceiling and ceaselessly scrutinizing the plasterwork for outlines of animals, human heads, signs.

All I can say of the actual process which allowed me to escape from these repetitive and burdensome acrobatics and gave me access to my own story and to my own voice, all I can say of it is that it was infinitely slow: it was the process of analysis itself, but I only realized that afterwards. What had to give way first was my armour – the hard shell of writing, beneath which my desire to write was hidden, had to crack; the high wall of prefabricated memories had to crumble; my sanctuaries of rationalization had to be reduced to dust. I had to go back on my tracks, to travel once more the path I had trod and of which I had lost the thread.

There is nothing I can say about that buried place. I know it had a place and that its trace is forevermore marked in me and in the texts that I write. It took the time that it took for my story to come together: a story that offered itself up to me one day – surprised, bewildered, forceful, like a memory restored to its own space, like a gesture or tenderness resurrected. That day the analyst heard what I had to say to him, what for four years he had listened to without hearing, for the simple reason that I hadn't been telling him that I wasn't saying it to myself.

1977

I Remember Malet & Isaac

I USED TO THINK I had forgotten nothing in my old school history books, but when I tried to summon up the memory of one or two chapter headings (The France of Louis XIV, The Great Discoveries, etc.), or some of the terms (defenestration of Prague, pragmatic sanction, Holy Alliance, continental blockade, the Augsburg Confession, rotten boroughs, peace of Pozsony, Treaty of Tilsit, Council of Trent, Brinvilliers affair, Field of the Cloth of Gold, etc.) or a picture or two (the peasant carrying an aristocrat and a cleric on his back, the map of the campaign of 1814, the woman with a coiffure in the shape of a caravel, etc.), I realized I was wrong, for almost none came back to mind. I had to search for some of those old school-books and find them (almost by accident) before a rapid perusal of their elaborate layouts, with paragraph headings, bolds, and italics announcing the immutable framework of a self-confident educational system, brought back to me a few centuries of our history as it has been regurgitated by several generations of schoolchildren.

The following transcription, which is just a game with cut-and-paste, a listing of chapter headings, captions, highlighted keywords and so on, seems to me to illustrate quite effectively the phantom history we were taught, in which events, ideas, and (great) men slot into place like pieces in a jigsaw puzzle.

HEADINGS
(Malet, *Contemporary Period*, Chapter XX)

EUROPEAN EXPANSION

I. THE FORMATION OF THE BRITISH COLONIAL EMPIRE

FORMATION OF THE BRITISH EMPIRE – THE CONQUEST OF INDIA – REVOLT OF THE SEPOYS – PRESENT-DAY INDIA – CONQUESTS RELATED TO INDIA – THE OCCUPATION OF EGYPT – CONQUEST OF EGYPTIAN SUDAN – THE BRITISH IN SOUTH AFRICA – RHODESIA – CONQUEST OF ORANGE STATE AND TRANSVAAL – WESTERN AFRICA, NIGERIA – THE COMMONWEALTH OF CANADA – THE COMMONWEALTH OF AUSTRALIA – BRITISH IMPERIALISM

II. THE FORMATION OF THE FRENCH COLONIAL EMPIRE

FORMATION OF THE FRENCH EMPIRE – ALGERIA BEFORE THE CONQUEST – CAUSES OF THE WAR – CAPTURE OF ALGIERS – LIMITED OCCUPATION – CONQUEST – CAPTURE OF CONSTANTINE – ABD-EL-KADER – BUGEAUD – CAPTURE OF LA SMALA: L'ISLY – END OF CONQUEST – OCCUPATION OF TUNISIA – FRANCE'S MISSION – FRENCH SUDAN

– ITS CONQUEST – SAHARA – FRENCH CONGO –
UNITY OF THE AFRICAN EMPIRE – MADAGASCAR –
CONQUEST – ACQUISITION OF COCHIN-CHINA –
FIRST CONQUEST OF TONKIN – WAR WITH CHINA
– PRESENT-DAY INDOCHINA – VALUE OF FRENCH
COLONIES

III. GERMAN EMIGRATION AND TRADE

GERMAN EMIGRATION – GERMAN COLONIES –
GERMAN INDUSTRY – GERMAN TRADE – MERCHANT
FLEET – TRADE POLICY – PAN-GERMANISM.

SUBHEADINGS
(Malet, *Modern History*, Lower Sixth Form, Chapter IX)

THE RENAISSANCE

ARTISTS, HUMANISTS AND WRITERS IN ITALY AND FRANCE

I. RENAISSANCE, CHARACTERISTICS OF

Causes of the Renaissance – Patrons

II. THE RENAISSANCE IN ITALY

Humanists – Writers – Artists – Painters – Leonardo
da Vinci – Bramante – Michelangelo – Michelangelo
the sculptor – Michelangelo the painter – Michelangelo the architect – Raphael – Andrea del Sarto –
Northern painters, characteristics of – Giorgione,
Titian – Correggio – Tintoretto, Veronese – Minor
Arts – Renaissance Morality

III. THE RENAISSANCE IN FRANCE

Nature of the French Renaissance – Humanism in
France – Collège de France – Writers in the time of
François I – Writers in the latter half of the century –
Artists – Painters – Architects – Architects of classical
inspiration – Blois, Le Lude and the Louvre – Sculp-
tors of the French tradition – Classical sculptors –
Minor Arts – Change in Artists' Standing

IV. THE RENAISSANCE IN GERMANY

Germany and Humanism – Erasmus – The Arts –
Albrecht Dürer – Holbein – Domination of Italy

ITALICS

(Malet, *Eighteenth Century, Revolution and Empire*
Sixth Form, Chapter XII: France in 1789)

Territorially
Politically absolute centralized The monarch speaks. All
are subjects and all subjects to obey me utterly muddled
administrative organization was not unified
Society inequality three classes the privileged classes
the unprivileged class
Hereditary king Salic law
divine right
absolute
arbitrary censorship confiscation lettre de cachet
military quarters civil quarters
the king's mouth
"The Court was the Nation's grave"
Chancellor General Controller of Finances The King's

Household Foreign Affairs War Navy Minister Prime Minister
    Supreme Court Higher Council Council of Finances
Emergency Council Council of the Parties
    Central Government
    Governments provinces provincial administrations
40 Governments governors
36 provinces provincial administrations centralized monarchy
    elections dioceses fiefdoms deputies
    was not a unified monarchy
    perch
    Regions of charter Electoral regions seven different rates salt tax
    Written law common law
    five large estates foreign provinces letters of credit
    "but an unconstituted aggregation of disunited peoples"
    Screeds
    seigneurial jurisdiction fiefdom seneschalsy Court of Assistance
    Presidials Parliaments
    recourse one third
    owners of their charges venality of charges
    Spices
    Preparatory questions prior questions
    "the king's expenditure cannot be related to his receipts but only to his expenses"
    what was extraordinary
    tax capitation twentieths
    tax property tax tax on income arbitrary tax on presumed income capitation
    twentieth tenth one fifth

"bought back" "subscribers" 1 in 100 – 1.1
10 in 100 – 9.9
At least half of what bourgeois, peasant or worker earned
went to the coffers of the State
   indirect taxes   salt tax   assistance   tax farmers   salt tax
redeemed land   free province   great   lesser salt tax   duty tax
   exciseman   illicit salt making
   assistance
   inequality   orders   Clergy   Nobility   Third Estate   the
privileged   honorary   real
   regular   secular   officialities
   impossible to estimate accurately   three thousand million
tithe   federal rights
   special tithes   free gift   oblate gift   one thousand five
hundred million
   high clergy   commissioners
   low clergy   priests or vicars   titular priests   large tithe-
owners   priests in charge of chapels of ease   the fitting portion
   nobility of the sword   nobility of the robe   ennobled
squires   courtly nobility   lower nobility   provincial nobility
   champart   tolls   common use   real privileges
   nobility of the robe
   "legal nobility"
   It was therefore directly affected by the financial crisis
political transformation
   equality   social reform   Sieyès
   colonizers   day-labourers   share-croppers   colonizer   day-
labourer   share-cropper   electors who had paid the poll tax
   "the state's donkey"   champart   common usage   champart
common usage
   three-quarters of his income   he was left with barely a

fifth of the fruit of his labour
one franc the kilogram

PICTURE AND CAPTION

(Malet, *Modern History*, p. 417)

CHARLES IX (1550–1574)
After the portrait by François Clouet
Musée du Louvre. Photograph by Braun.

Charles IX is nineteen years old: he is pallid, his eyes are yellow, his eyebrows blond, as is his hair, and he wears a wispy moustache and short, sparse side-whiskers. He has an intelligent face, but with something unsteady and anxious about it betraying his jumpy, weak-willed character, easily aroused and easily dominated. – This portrait with its miniaturist's precision is one of the best works of François Clouet, the only important painter of the French Renaissance. It depicts a very pretty kind of late sixteenth-century costume, consisting of a black velvet doublet with goffered ruff and loose wing-sleeves delicately embroidered with gold thread; a jerkin (only the sleeves can be seen) and bouffant breeches in gold-flecked white satin, with tight-fitting hose. The necklace is of pearls and openwork gold balls finished off with a cross. – A black velvet cap is worn down to the ear and one side, and decorated with a ruby and plume of white feathers. The red armchair is Henri II in style, with silver frogging, fringes, and studs. The curtains are of green satin.

BOLD

(Malet & Isaac, *The World in the Nineteenth Century,*
Advanced Primary Level, Year 3.
General Review, pp. 280–309)

Modern nations in Western Europe France Philip-
Augustus Saint-Louis Philippe the Fair Charles VII
Louis XI
    England Magna Carta Parliament
    Spain marriage
    Germany Austrian Habsburgs the elective crown
    Great seafaring inventions and discoveries compass
gunpowder rag paper printing Diaz 1487 Vasco da
Gama 1498 Christopher Columbus 1492 Magellan
    The humanist Renaissance Copernicus Vinci
Michelangelo Raphael châteaux Marot Rabelais Ron-
sard Montaigne
    Reform Luther Calvin Anglicanism The Council of
Trent The Society of Jesus
    French Monarchy from 1498 to 1559 Louis XII
François I Henri II court absolute sovereigns Concordat
privy council
    The struggle against the house of Austria Italian wars
Marignano the empire of Charles V Pavia the treaty of
Cateau-Cambrésis
    The wars of religion Catherine de' Medici Michel de
l'Hôpital François de Guise the Saint Bartholomew's
Day massacre Coligny Holy League Henry de Guise
Philippe II Henry IV the Edict of Nantes
    Restoration of royal authority Richelieu Mazarin
Fronde

Absolute monarchy Louis XIV

Religious questions in the seventeenth century the pardon of Alais the revocation of the Edict of Nantes Jansenists

French preponderance in seventeenth century in Europe Thirty Years' War Gustavus-Adolphus Condé Turenne Treaty of Westphalia Treaty of Pyrenees War of Devolution Dutch War War of the Augsburg League the War of the Spanish Succession Utrecht

French economic life in the seventeenth century Corneille Racine Descartes Pascal Molière La Fontaine Bossuet Velásquez Rubens Rembrandt Kepler Descartes Pascal Galileo Huygens Leibnitz Newton

France and Europe in 1715 William of Orange Kingdom of Prussia Peter the Great Russian power

France under Louis XV Regency Law Cardinal Fleury Pompadour Du Barry conflicts with Parliament

New ideas Locke Montesquieu Voltaire Diderot Rousseau the salons the Encyclopædia economists enlightened despotism Joseph II

French foreign policy in the eighteenth century War of the Polish Succession War of the Austrian Succession Fontenoy Frederick II the reversal of alliances Dupleix The Seven Years' War Rosbach Leuthen partition of Poland voyages of exploration Cook

Louis XVI the onset of Revolution Turgot American War Washington independence of the United States Necker financial crisis Estates General

General causes of the French Revolution France in 1789 unequal burden of taxation feudal rights

The Estates General; the Constituent Assembly (1789–1791) 17 June National Assembly 20 June the

oath of the Jeu de Paume Constituent Assembly 14 July
the night of 4 August Declaration of the Rights of Man
5–6 October Fête de la Fédération civil status of the
clergy the king tries to flee

The Legislative Assembly and the war (1791–1792)
Girondins Jacobins 20 April 1792 the Girondin ministry
declares war 20 June 1792 Brunswick manifesto the
day of 10 August September massacres Valmy

The Convention (1792–1795) Abolition of royalty
Girondins Montagnards Jemmapes coalition Vendée
Revolutionary Government Robespierre Reign of Terror
Carnot Fleurus 9 Thermidor Treaties of Bâle and The
Hague establishment of schools 1793 Constitution
Constitution of Year III

The Directoire (1795–1799) Bonaparte Italian campaign Peace of Campo Formio coup d'état of 18 Fructi-
dor coup d'état of 22 Floréal Egyptian expedition
second coalition Zürich coup d'état of 18–19 Brumaire

The Napoleonic Regime (1799–1815) Constitution
of the Year VIII Consulate Life Consul Emperor
Napoleon I administrative reorganization Civil Code
Concordat

Napoleon's foreign policy Marengo Hohenlinden
Treaty of Lunéville Treaty of Amiens Camp of Boulogne
Third Coalition Ulm Austerlitz Trafalgar Peace of
Pozsony Fourth Coalition Auerstaedt Continental
Blockade Eylau Friedland Treaty of Tilsit Spanish War
Fifth Coalition Wagram Treaty of Vienna Moscow
retreat from Russia Seventh Coalition Leipzig French
Campaign abdicate

The Restoration and the Hundred Days Treaty of

Paris Congress of Vienna Hundred Days Waterloo abdicate Second Treaty of Paris

The Government of the Restoration (1815–1830) 1814 Charter ultras independent constitutional party White Terror Decazes Charles X July Ordinances Revolution of 27, 28, 29 July

The July Monarchy (1830–1848) revised 1814 charter legitimists republicans party of resistance Guizot catholic and socialist parties Revolution of February 1848

French foreign policy from 1815 to 1848 Holy Alliance Metternich Navarin entente cordiale Belgian independence Eastern crisis of 1840 expedition to seize Algiers limited occupation Abd-el-Kader extended occupation Constantine total conquest Bugeaud Isly

Literature, the arts and science in France in the first half of the nineteenth century romanticism classicism Chateaubriand Lamartine Victor Hugo Vigny Musset Balzac George Sand Augustin Thierry Michelet David Ingres Géricault Delacroix Rude Barye mechanisation heavy industry steamships railways electric telegraph socialists

The Second Republic (1848–1851) provisional government moderate socialists national workhouses Constituent Assembly 15 May June Days 1848 Constitution Louis-Napoleon Legislative Assembly the Falloux Act coup d'état of 2 December 1851

The Second Empire (1852–1870) Emperor Napoleon III 1852 Constitution Authoritarian Empire Liberal Empire third-party Olivier's parliamentary government Revolution of 4 September 1870

Napoleon III's foreign policy Crimean War Sebastopol

Congress of Paris Italian War Magena Solferino
cession of Nice and Savoy Roman question Mexican
war Sadowa
The war of 1870 the Ems telegram Moltke Froesch-
willer Rezonville Saint-Privat Sedan government of
national defence Paris capitulation Beaune-la-Rolande
Loigny Champigny Mans Saint-Quentin Héricourt
Buzenval Treaty of Frankfurt
Third Republic National Assembly Thiers 18 March
Commune Bloody Week liberation of territory seven-
year term moral order 1875 Constitution parliamen-
tary republic 16 May 1877 school laws of Jules Ferry
Formation of a new French colonial empire Algeria
Tunisia Senegal Sudan French Congo Madagascar
Cochin-china Cambodia Tonkin Annam
Development of science in France in the second half of
the nineteenth century Sainte-Claire Deville Wurtz
Pasteur Berthelot Claude Bernard Pasteur Renard
aviation
Europe after 1815, the Holy Alliance Holy Alliance
Metternich politics of congress and intervention Con-
gresses of Karlsbad and Vienna Laybach and Verona
Congresses Revolution of 1830 Belgian independence
Italian unity (1859–1870) 1848 Custozza Novare
Cavour victorious war against Austria (1859) Garibaldi
king of Italy Veneto Roman Question
German unity (1866–1871) 1848 Parliament of Frank-
furt Restricted Union withdrawal of Olmütz Bismarck
the affair of the duchies Sadowa North German Confed-
eration war against France German Emperor
The Eastern question in the nineteenth century
Serbian insurrection Greek insurrection Russo-Turkish

war Egyptian affair Crimean War Balkan War Congress
of Berlin Bulgarian unity Greco-Turkish War Turkish
Revolution
   Contemporary Europe: alliances and armed peace
alliance of the three emperors Anglo-French alliance
armed peace
   Origins of the constitutional monarchy 1688 Revolu-
tion sovereignty of the people parliamentary American
Revolution French Revolution
   Parliamentary monarchy; England reforms of 1832
Irish question
   French and Swiss Republics France 1875 Parliamen-
tary Republic Switzerland direct government
   American and Australian Republics United States
immigration War of Secession Monroe doctrine Latin
America independence civil wars Republic of the
Argentine development of democratic institutions
socialist-inspired legislation
   Federal monarchies, Germany and Austria-Hungary
Germany Bismarck catholic party Kulturkampf social-
ist party Wilhelm II Alsace-Lorraine Austria-Hungary
national aspirations dual crown Czechs
   The last absolute monarchies Russia autocracy
Nicholas I, Alexander II, emancipation of the serfs
terrorist party 1905 revolutionary agitation Turkey
two revolutions 1876 1908 China patriarchal despotism Republic Japan feudal monarchy Shogun
1868 Revolution
   Economic Transformation heavy industry railways
steamships telegraph telephone wireless telegraph
paper money protectionist regime
   Partition of Africa Berlin conference France

Morocco England Boers Boer War Egypt Belgium Independent State of Congo Germany Spain Portugal Italy

Europeans in Asia English Conquest of India Russians Central Asia France opium war Franco-British expedition Korean War Boxer uprising Manchurian War

Colonial policy autonomous colonies the native question major rail routes

Social evolution slave trading slavery serfdom black question agrarian question religious freedom separation of Church and State free compulsory primary education compulsory military service

Socialist movement socialist doctrines socialist parties cooperative unions workers' legislation

1979

81 Easy-Cook Recipes for Beginners

Sole aux champignons

Take two fine whole fresh sole, skin and fillet them. Bake in a medium oven for 40 minutes, basting frequently. When half-done, add a half-pound of button mushrooms. Lay out on a heated serving dish and sprinkle generously with ground fennel.

Lapin au Noilly

Smear a pair of small rabbits with a generous coating of full-strength mustard. Cook in a casserole together with a few rashers of bacon, sliced carrots, fresh tomatoes and spring onions. To make the gravy, add a dash of vermouth to the liquid. Serve with ratatouille.

Ris de veau "à ma façon"

Take four sweetbreads, soak in lemon water, then drain and cut into thin slices. Bake in a medium oven for 40 minutes, basting frequently. Remove from heat and then add two tablespoons of double cream. Serve with stiffly beaten egg whites.

SOLE À LA CRÈME

Take two fine whole fresh sole, skin and fillet them. Cook in a casserole together with a few rashers of bacon, sliced carrots, fresh tomatoes and spring onions. Remove from heat and then add two tablespoons of double cream. Lay out on a heated serving dish and sprinkle generously with tarragon.

RIS DE VEAU FLAMANDE

Take four sweetbreads, soak in lemon water, then drain and cut into thin slices. Brown the sweetbreads in a hot shallow pan, then lower the heat and leave to simmer. When half done, add a half-pound of button mushrooms. Lay out on a heated serving dish and sprinkle generously with soft brown sugar.

LAPIN À LA BOURGUIGNONNE

Smear a pair of small rabbits with a generous coating of full-strength mustard. Bake in a medium oven for 40 minutes, basting frequently. To make the gravy, add a dash of vermouth to the liquid. Serve with a jug of *sauce bourguignonne*.

RIS DE VEAU GRAND-MÈRE

Take four sweetbreads, soak in lemon water, then drain and cut into thin slices. Cook in a casserole together with a few rashers of bacon, sliced carrots, fresh tomatoes and spring onions. When half done, add a half-pound of button mushrooms. Serve with a jug of caper sauce.

LAPEREAU À LA MOUTARDE

Smear a pair of small rabbits with a generous coating of full-strength mustard. Bake in a medium oven for 40 minutes, basting frequently. When half done, add a half-pound of button mushrooms. Serve with potato pancakes.

SOLE AU NOILLY

Take two fine whole fresh sole, skin and fillet them. Cook in a casserole together with a few rashers of bacon, sliced carrots, fresh tomatoes and spring onions. To make the gravy, add a dash of vermouth to the liquid. Lay out on a heated serving dish and sprinkle generously with fresh thyme.

RIS DE VEAU À LA CRÈME

Take four sweetbreads, soak in lemon water, then drain and cut into thin slices. Brown the sweetbreads in a hot shallow pan, then lower the heat and leave to simmer. Remove from heat and then add two tablespoons of double cream. Serve with a jug of mousseline sauce.

LAPIN AUX NAVETS

Smear a pair of small rabbits with a generous coating of full-strength mustard. Cook in a casserole together with a few rashers of bacon, sliced carrots, fresh tomatoes and spring onions. When half done, add a half-pound of button mushrooms. Serve with glacé turnips.

SOLE AU FOUR

Take two fine whole fresh sole, skin and fillet them. Bake in a medium oven for 40 minutes, basting frequently. To make the gravy, add a dash of vermouth to the liquid. Serve with a jug of white-butter sauce.

SOLE PRINTANIÈRE

Take two fine whole fresh sole, skin and fillet them. Cook in a casserole together with a few rashers of bacon, sliced carrots, fresh tomatoes and spring onions. Remove from heat and then add two tablespoons of double cream. Serve with peas.

Ris de veau aux champignons

Take four sweetbreads, soak in lemon water, then drain and cut into thin slices. Bake in a medium oven for 40 minutes, basting frequently. When half done, add a half-pound of button mushrooms. Lay out on a heated serving dish and sprinkle generously with chives.

Lapin au roquefort

Smear a pair of small rabbits with a generous coating of full-strength mustard. Cook in a casserole together with a few rashers of bacon, sliced carrots, fresh tomatoes and spring onions. Remove from heat and then add two tablespoons of double cream. Lay out on a heated serving dish and sprinkle generously with crumbled Roquefort cheese.

Lapin à la saigonnaise

Smear a pair of small rabbits with a generous coating of full-strength mustard. Bake in a medium oven for 40 minutes, basting frequently. Remove from heat and then add two tablespoons of double cream. Serve with a jug of *nuoc mam*.

Sole à l'oseille

Take two fine whole fresh sole, skin and fillet them. Brown the fish in a hot shallow pan, then lower the heat and leave to simmer. To make the gravy, add a dash of vermouth to the liquid. Serve with mashed sorrel leaves.

Ris de veau béarnaise

Take four sweetbreads, soak in lemon water, then drain

and cut into thin slices. Cook in a casserole together with a few rashers of bacon, sliced carrots, fresh tomatoes and spring onions. To make the gravy, add a dash of vermouth to the liquid. Serve with a jug of Béarnaise sauce.

LAPIN AUX CARDONS

Smear a pair of small rabbits with a generous coating of full-strength mustard. Brown them in a hot shallow pan, then lower the heat and leave to simmer. When half done, add a half-pound of button mushrooms. Serve with shrimps.

SOLES CHORON

Take two fine whole fresh sole, skin and fillet them. Brown the fish in a hot shallow pan, then lower the heat and leave to simmer. When half done, add a half-pound of button mushrooms. Serve with a jug of Choron sauce.

RIS DE VEAU À L'ITALIENNE

Take four sweetbreads, soak in lemon water, then drain and cut into thin slices. Bake in a medium oven for 40 minutes, basting frequently. To make the gravy, add a dash of vermouth to the liquid. Lay out on a heated serving dish and sprinkle generously with Parmesan cheese.

SOLES À L'ÉTOUFFÉE

Take two fine whole fresh sole, skin and fillet them. Cook in a casserole together with a few rashers of bacon, sliced carrots, fresh tomatoes and spring onions. When half done, add a half-pound of button mushrooms. Lay out on a heated serving dish and sprinkle generously with rosemary.

LAPEREAUX À LA MOSCOVITE

Smear a pair of small rabbits with a generous coating of full-strength mustard. Brown them in a hot shallow pan, then lower the heat and leave to simmer. Remove from heat and then add two tablespoons of double cream. Serve with a jug of devil's sauce.

Sole "sans-façon"

Take two fine whole fresh sole, skin and fillet them. Bake in a medium oven for 40 minutes, basting frequently. Remove from heat and then add two tablespoons of double cream. Lay out on a heated serving dish and sprinkle generously with *fines herbes*.

Ris de veau Curnonsky

Take four sweetbreads, soak in lemon water, then drain and cut into thin slices. Brown the sweetbreads in a hot shallow pan, then lower the heat and leave to simmer. To make the gravy, add a dash of vermouth to the liquid. Serve with broccoli.

Lapin aux chipolatas

Smear a pair of small rabbits with a generous coating of full-strength mustard. Brown them in a hot shallow pan, then lower the heat and leave to simmer. To make the gravy, add a dash of vermouth to the liquid. Serve with chipolatas.

Soles Soubise

Take two fine whole fresh sole, skin and fillet them. Brown the fish in a hot shallow pan, then lower the heat and leave to simmer. Remove from heat and then add two tablespoons of double cream. Serve with a jug of Soubise sauce.

Ris de veau en cocotte

Take four sweetbreads, soak in lemon water, then drain and cut into thin slices. Cook in a casserole together with a few rashers of bacon, sliced carrots, fresh tomatoes and spring onions. Remove from heat and then add two table-spoons of double cream. Serve with artichoke hearts.

LAPIN À LA PISTACHE

Smear a pair of small rabbits with a generous coating of full-strength mustard. Bake in a medium oven for 40 minutes, basting frequently. Remove from heat and then add two tablespoons of double cream. Lay out on a heated serving dish and sprinkle generously with ground pistachios.

RIS DE VEAU AURORE

Take four sweetbreads, soak in lemon water, then drain and cut into thin slices. Brown them in a hot shallow pan, then lower the heat and leave to simmer. To make the gravy, add a dash of vermouth to the liquid. Serve with a jug of Aurora sauce.

LAPIN AU CUMIN

Smear a pair of small rabbits with a generous coating of full-strength mustard. Brown them in a hot shallow pan, then lower the heat and leave to simmer. When half done, add a half-pound of button mushrooms. Lay out on a heated serving dish and sprinkle generously with cumin.

SUPRÊME DE SOLE

Take two fine whole fresh sole, skin and fillet them. Bake in a medium oven for 40 minutes, basting frequently. When half done, add a half-pound of button mushrooms. Serve with asparagus.

RIS DE VEAU À LA SEYCHELLOISE

Take four sweetbreads, soak in lemon water, then drain and cut into thin slices. Brown the sweetbreads in a hot shallow pan, then lower the heat and leave to simmer.

Remove from heat and then add two tablespoons of double cream. Lay out on a heated serving dish and sprinkle generously with grated coconut.

LAPIN À LA PROVENÇALE

Smear a pair of small rabbits with a generous coating of full-strength mustard. Cook in a casserole together with a few rashers of bacon, sliced carrots, fresh tomatoes and spring onions. When half done, add a half-pound of button mushrooms. Serve with aioli.

RIS DE VEAU SURPRISE

Take four sweetbreads, soak in lemon water, then drain and cut into thin slices. Bake in a medium oven for 40 minutes, basting frequently. To make the gravy, add a dash of vermouth to the liquid. Serve with a tea sorbet.

SOLE BRAISÉE AUVERGNATE

Take two fine whole fresh sole, skin and fillet them. Cook in a casserole together with a few rashers of bacon, sliced carrots, fresh tomatoes and spring onions. To make the gravy, add a dash of vermouth to the liquid. Serve with lentils.

RIS DE VEAU MÉPHISTO

Take four sweetbreads, soak in lemon water, then drain and cut into thin slices. Bake in a medium oven for 40 minutes, basting frequently. When half done, add a half-pound of button mushrooms. Serve with chili sauce.

SOLE "CAFÉ DE PARIS"

Take two fine whole fresh sole, skin and fillet them. Cook in a casserole together with a few rashers of bacon, sliced carrots, fresh tomatoes and spring onions. When half done, add a half-pound of button mushrooms. Serve with a jug of Béchamel sauce.

Lapin au basilic

Smear a pair of small rabbits with a generous coating of full-strength mustard. Bake in a medium oven for 40 minutes, basting frequently. When half done, add a half-pound of button mushrooms. Lay out on a heated serving dish and sprinkle generously with basil.

Ris de veau à la lyonnaise

Take four sweetbreads, soak in lemon water, then drain and cut into thin slices. Cook in a casserole together with a few rashers of bacon, sliced carrots, fresh tomatoes and spring onions. Remove from heat and then add two tablespoons of double cream. Serve with a jug of sauce ravigote.

Lapereau sauté "Val d'Aoste"

Smear a pair of small rabbits with a generous coating of full-strength mustard. Brown them in a hot shallow pan, then lower the heat and leave to simmer. To make the gravy, add a dash of vermouth to the liquid. Lay out on a heated serving dish and sprinkle generously with star anise.

Filets de sole bruxelloise

Take two fine whole fresh sole, skin and fillet them. Brown the fish in a hot shallow pan, then lower the heat and leave to simmer. When half done, add a half-pound of button mushrooms. Serve with a jug of Hollandaise sauce.

Sole charcutière

Take two fine whole fresh sole, skin and fillet them. Bake in a medium oven for 40 minutes, basting frequently.

Remove from heat and then add two tablespoons of double cream. Serve with applesauce.

Ris de veau au safran

Take four sweetbreads, soak in lemon water, then drain and cut into thin slices. Bake in a medium oven for 40 minutes, basting frequently. Remove from heat and then add two tablespoons of double cream. Lay out on a heated serving dish and sprinkle generously with saffron.

Lapin à l'alsacienne

Smear a pair of small rabbits with a generous coating of full-strength mustard. Cook in a casserole together with a few rashers of bacon, sliced carrots, fresh tomatoes and spring onions. Remove from heat and then add two tablespoons of double cream. Serve with fresh pasta.

Ris de veau Saint-Sylvestre

Take four sweetbreads, soak in lemon water, then drain and cut into thin slices. Brown the sweetbreads in a hot shallow pan, then lower the heat and leave to simmer. When half done, add a half-pound of button mushrooms. Serve with hot chestnuts.

Filets de sole basse-calorie

Take two fine whole fresh sole, skin and fillet them. Bake in a medium oven for 40 minutes, basting frequently. To make the gravy, add a dash of vermouth to the liquid. Serve with white beets.

Ris de veau périgourdine

Take four sweetbreads, soak in lemon water, then drain and cut into thin slices. Cook in a casserole together with a few rashers of bacon, sliced carrots, fresh tomatoes and spring onions. When half done, add a half-pound of button mushrooms. Serve with mashed celery.

LAPIN AUX AMANDES

Smear a pair of small rabbits with a generous coating of full-strength mustard. Bake in a medium oven for 40 minutes, basting frequently. To make the gravy, add a dash of vermouth to the liquid. Lay out on a heated serving dish and sprinkle generously with crushed almonds.

SOLE LANDAISE

Take two fine whole fresh sole, skin and fillet them. Brown the fish in a hot shallow pan, then lower the heat and leave to simmer. Remove from heat and then add two tablespoons of double cream. Serve with baked eggplants.

LAPIN À LA TOURGANELLE

Smear a pair of small rabbits with a generous coating of full-strength mustard. Cook in a casserole together with a few rashers of bacon, sliced carrots, fresh tomatoes and spring onions. To make the gravy, add a dash of vermouth to the liquid. Serve with a jug of tomato sauce.

RIS DE VEAU FLAMANDE

Take four sweetbreads, soak in lemon water, then drain and cut into thin slices. Brown the sweetbreads in a hot shallow pan, then lower the heat and leave to simmer. When half done, add a half-pound of button mushrooms. Serve with mayonnaise.

LAPEREAU À LA HONGROISE

Smear a pair of small rabbits with a generous coating of full-strength mustard. Brown them in a hot shallow pan, then lower the heat and leave to simmer. Remove from heat and then add two tablespoons of double cream. Lay out on a heated serving dish and sprinkle generously with paprika.

Sole bonne-femme

Take two fine whole fresh sole, skin and fillet them. Brown the fish in a hot shallow pan, then lower the heat and leave to simmer. When half done, add a half-pound of button mushrooms. Serve with Vichy carrots.

Ris de veau Louis XIV

Take four sweetbreads, soak in lemon water, then drain and cut into thin slices. Cook in a casserole together with a few rashers of bacon, sliced carrots, fresh tomatoes and spring onions. To make the gravy, add a dash of vermouth to the liquid. Lay out on a heated serving dish and sprinkle generously with chervil.

Sole à l'anglaise

Take two fine whole fresh sole, skin and fillet them. Bake in a medium oven for 40 minutes, basting frequently. When half done, add a half-pound of button mushrooms. Serve with a jug of horseradish sauce.

Lapin aux cacahuètes

Smear a pair of small rabbits with a generous coating of full-strength mustard. Cook in a casserole together with a few rashers of bacon, sliced carrots, fresh tomatoes and spring onions. To make the gravy, add a dash of vermouth to the liquid. Lay out on a heated serving dish and sprinkle generously with pulverized peanuts.

Ris au riz

Take four sweetbreads, soak in lemon water, then drain and cut into thin slices. Bake in a medium oven for 40 minutes, basting frequently. When half done, add a half-pound of button mushrooms. Serve with rice pudding.

Sole aux échalotes

Take two fine whole fresh sole, skin and fillet them. Brown the fish in a hot shallow pan, then lower the heat and leave to simmer. To make the gravy, add a dash of vermouth to the liquid. Lay out on a heated serving dish and sprinkle generously with chopped shallots.

Lapereau Bercy

Smear a pair of small rabbits with a generous coating of full-strength mustard. Brown them in a hot shallow pan, then lower the heat and leave to simmer. When half done, add a half-pound of button mushrooms. Serve with a jug of Bercy sauce.

Ris de veau bernoise

Take four sweetbreads, soak in lemon water, then drain and cut into thin slices. Cook in a casserole together with a few rashers of bacon, sliced carrots, fresh tomatoes and spring onions. Remove from heat and then add two table-spoons of double cream. Lay out on a heated serving dish and sprinkle generously with Gruyère cheese.

Lapereaux "Happy Few"

Smear a pair of small rabbits with a generous coating of full-strength mustard. Brown them in a hot shallow pan, then lower the heat and leave to simmer. To make the gravy, add a dash of vermouth to the liquid. Serve with custard.

Sole strasbourgeoise

Take two fine whole fresh sole, skin and fillet them. Brown the fish in a hot shallow pan, then lower the heat and leave to simmer. Remove from heat and then add two table-spoons of double cream. Lay out on a heated serving dish and sprinkle generously with fried parsley.

LAPIN BRAISÉ

Smear a pair of small rabbits with a generous coating of full-strength mustard. Cook in a casserole together with a few rashers of bacon, sliced carrots, fresh tomatoes and spring onions. Remove from heat and then add two table-spoons of double cream. Serve with a jug of white sauce.

SOLE À LA PAIMPOLAISE

Take two fine whole fresh sole, skin and fillet them. Cook in a casserole together with a few rashers of bacon, sliced carrots, fresh tomatoes and spring onions. When half done, add a half-pound of button mushrooms. Serve with baked cauliflower.

RIS DE VEAU PRINCESSE

Take four sweetbreads, soak in lemon water, then drain and cut into thin slices. Bake in a medium oven for 40 min-utes, basting frequently. Remove from heat and then add two tablespoons of double cream. Serve with a jug of Mor-nay sauce.

SOLE MAÎTRE D'HÔTEL

Take two fine whole fresh sole, skin and fillet them. Cook in a casserole together with a few rashers of bacon, sliced carrots, fresh tomatoes and spring onions. To make the gravy, add a dash of vermouth to the liquid. Serve with a jug of maître-d'hôtel sauce.

LAPIN RÔTI GRENOBLOISE

Smear a pair of small rabbits with a generous coating of

full-strength mustard. Bake in a medium oven for 40 minutes, basting frequently. To make the gravy, add a dash of vermouth to the liquid. Serve with Savoy potatoes.

RIS DE VEAU À LA PURÉE DE CRESSON

Take four sweetbreads, soak in lemon water, then drain and cut into thin slices. Brown the sweetbreads in a hot shallow pan, then lower the heat and leave to simmer. Remove from heat and then add two tablespoons of double cream. Serve with a watercress purée.

SOLES STRAVINSKY

Take two fine whole fresh sole, skin and fillet them. Cook in a casserole together with a few rashers of bacon, sliced carrots, fresh tomatoes and spring onions. Remove from heat and then add two tablespoons of double cream. Serve with a jug of Bordelaise sauce.

LAPEREAU "VILLA D'OUEST"

Smear a pair of small rabbits with a generous coating of full-strength mustard. Bake in a medium oven for 40 minutes, basting frequently. When half done, add a half-pound of button mushrooms. Serve with tartar sauce.

SOLE À L'ANCIENNE

Take two fine whole fresh sole, skin and fillet them. Bake in a medium oven for 40 minutes, basting frequently. To make the gravy, add a dash of vermouth to the liquid. Lay out on a heated serving dish and sprinkle generously with grated nutmeg.

RIS DE VEAU À L'AMÉRICAINE

Take four sweetbreads, soak in lemon water, then drain and cut into thin slices. Cook in a casserole together with a few rashers of bacon, sliced carrots, fresh tomatoes and spring onions. When half done, add a half-pound of button mushrooms. Lay out on a heated serving dish and sprinkle generously with cayenne pepper.

Lapin "Sans Souci"

Smear a pair of small rabbits with a generous coating of full-strength mustard. Bake in a medium oven for 40 minutes, basting frequently. Remove from heat and then add two tablespoons of double cream. Serve with steamed potatoes.

Ris de veau grand-seigneur

Take four sweetbreads, soak in lemon water, then drain and cut into thin slices. Brown the sweetbreads in a hot shallow pan, then lower the heat and leave to simmer. To make the gravy, add a dash of vermouth to the liquid. Lay out on a heated serving dish and sprinkle generously with finely shredded lemon rind.

Ris de veau au Noilly

Take four sweetbreads, soak in lemon water, then drain and cut into thin slices. Bake in a medium oven for 40 minutes, basting frequently. To make the gravy, add a dash of vermouth to the liquid. Serve with rémoulade sauce.

Sole exotique

Take two fine whole fresh sole, skin and fillet them. Brown the fish in a hot shallow pan, then lower the heat and leave to simmer. When half done, add a half-pound of button mushrooms. Lay out on a heated serving dish and sprinkle generously with cinnamon.

Lapin "Grand Hôtel de Paris"

Smear a pair of small rabbits with a generous coating of

full-strength mustard. Brown them in a hot shallow pan, then lower the heat and leave to simmer. Remove from heat and then add two tablespoons of double cream. Serve with fried salsify.

SOLE AU FOUR À LA NORMANDE

Take two fine whole fresh sole, skin and fillet them. Bake in a medium oven for 40 minutes, basting frequently. Remove from heat and then add two tablespoons of double cream. Serve with a jug of melted butter.

RIS DE VEAU BRAISÉ "YORKSHIRE"

Take four sweetbreads, soak in lemon water, then drain and cut into thin slices. Cook in a casserole together with a few rashers of bacon, sliced carrots, fresh tomatoes and spring onions. To make the gravy, add a dash of vermouth to the liquid. Serve with Yorkshire pudding.

LAPIN BERRICHON

Smear a pair of small rabbits with a generous coating of full-strength mustard. Cook in a casserole together with a few rashers of bacon, sliced carrots, fresh tomatoes and spring onions. When half done, add a half-pound of button mushrooms. Lay out on a heated serving dish and sprinkle generously with breadcrumbs.

1980

READING

A SOCIO-PHYSIOLOGICAL SKETCH

THE FOLLOWING PAGES make no pretence of being more than notes – an intuitive, rather than an organized, compilation of disparate facts which (with a few exceptions) pertain to no constituted body of knowledge, but rather to the ill-mapped, unfarmed fields of descriptive ethnology, as Marcel Mauss described them in his introduction to "body techniques": that is to say, those kinds of facts usually referred to as "miscellaneous," because all we know about them is that we don't know very much, apart from the intuition that a good deal could be gleaned from them if we decided to pay them more attention.* For the plain and obvious facts that we don't bother about or acknowledge, the kinds of things that "go without saying" – these facts, though we may like to think that we don't have to describe them, describe us nonetheless. They speak with more relevance and substance than sociologists' habitual, institutional and ideological fare of the history of our bodies, the culture that

* Marcel Mauss, *Sociology and Psychology*, transl. Ben Brewster. London: Routledge, 1979, pp. 95–123.

has shaped our ways of moving and holding ourselves, the education which has moulded our motor, as well as our mental habits. As Mauss specified, they include our ways of walking, dancing, running, jumping, resting, carrying, and throwing; table manners, sexual mores, external marks of respect, rules of hygiene, etc. They also include the ways we read.

Reading is an act. I would like to talk exclusively about the act of reading – what constitutes it as an act, what settings it occurs in – and not at all about its product (a reading, a text read) or what precedes it (writing and the choices involved, publishing decisions, printing decisions, distribution decisions, and so on); in brief, I want to explore something like an economy of reading seen from an ergological angle (physiology, muscular movements) and from a socio-ecological perspective (its spatio-temporal environment).

A school of criticism of some decades' standing stresses the "how" of writing, its praxis and *poïesis*. It deals not with maieutics, the sacralised myth of the tousle-haired poet's inspiration, but with black on white, the texture, inscription and trace of the text, the letter in itself, craft at the microscopic level, the spatial arrangement of writing, the writer's tools (pen, brush, typewriter) and his working surfaces (Valmont to Madame de Tourvel, in Letter forty-eight of *Les Liaisons dangereuses*: "The very table on which I write this, never before put to such use, has become in my eyes the altar of love. ..."), writing codes such as punctuation marks, line spacing, line breaks, etc., and the writer's environment – where the writer writes, in what places, at what rhythm; writers who write in cafés, writers who write at night and those who rise at dawn, writers who work on Sundays, etc.).

A parallel study is needed, in my view, on the reciprocal activity of reading, on how readers appropriate written texts. We must try to grasp not the message received, but the receiving of the message at an elementary level, that is to say: What happens when you read. Eyes alight on lines and move about, but many other things accompany the movement. We must reduce reading to what it is in the first place: a particular activity of the body, the use of particular muscles, various postural arrangements, sequential decisions, time-constrained choices, and a set of strategies embedded in the continuum of social life. You don't just read anyhow, any time, any place, even if you read just anything.

I. The Body

Eyes

Reading is done with the eyes.* What eyes do when reading is a subject of a complexity well beyond my competence and the scope of this article. The copious literature produced on the matter since the beginning of the century (Yarbus,

---

* Except by the blind, who read with their fingers. With the further exception of people being read to: in Russian novels, duchesses with their ladies-in-waiting, who are often French girls ruined by the Revolution; or in novels by Erckmann-Chatrian, illiterate peasants who foregather of an evening (heavy wooden table, wooden bowls, pitchers, cat curled up on the hearth, dogs by the door) around one of them reading aloud a letter from a son wounded in battle, or the newspaper, the Bible or the almanac; or again, Maurice's grandparents whom Alphonse Daudet visits when an orphan girl is reading out the life of Saint Irene syllable by syllable.

Stark, etc.), allows us to be sure at least of one fundamental, if elementary, thing: eyes do not read letters one after the other, nor do they read whole words one after the other, nor lines one after the other, but proceed in spurts and stops, exploring simultaneously the whole visual field of reading with dogged redundancy: ceaseless movements punctuated by minute halts, as if, in order to find what is sought, the eye had to sweep the page with intense agitation, not in regular fashion like a television tube (and as the term "sweeping" would seem to suggest), but in an aleatory, muddled, and repetitive fashion, or, if you like, since we're deep in images anyway, like a pigeon pecking the ground as it hunts for breadcrumbs. The comparison is obviously a little suspect, but it nonetheless seems to me to characterize reading, and I do not hesitate to extrapolate from it something that could be the starting-point of a theory of the text: reading is first of all the extraction from a text of signifying elements, of meaning-crumbs, of something like the keywords which are made out, compared, and relocated. It's by checking that the keywords are there that you know you're in the text, that you can identify it and guarantee what it is; the keywords can be words (in detective stories, for example; even more so in erotic, or purportedly erotic, writing), but can also be sound effects (rhymes), lay-out features, turns of phrase, typographical conventions (for instance, the italicization of certain *words* in *far too many* contemporary works of fiction, criticism, and critical fiction), or even whole narrative sequences.*

---

* cf. Jacques Duchâteau, "A Marginal Reading of Peter Cheyney", in *La Littérature potentielle*. Paris: Gallimard, 1973.

What is involved is to some degree what information theory refers to as pattern-recognition: we seek out distinctive features allowing us to pass from what a text is in the first place – a linear sequence of letters, spaces and punctuation marks – to what its meaning will be once we have identified some syntactic coherence, some narrative structure, and something that is called a "style".

Beyond a few classic cases of an elementary, that is to say lexical, kind (reading is knowing without thinking that the word "fit" refers either to what an epileptic has or to what you seek in a glove or shoe, that Egyptian mummies raised no kids and that the tablets of the law are not to be swallowed whole), I really do not know what experimental procedures could be used to study these processes of recognition. For my part I only know of negative proofs – the feeling of intense frustration which for years overcame me when I read Russian novels (... *after the death of Anna Mikhailovna Drubetskoy, Boris Timofeyich Ismailov sought the hand of Katerina Lvovna Borissich, who spurned him for Ivan Mikhailov Vassiliev...*), or when at the age of fifteen I wanted to decipher the reputedly pornographic passages of Diderot's *Bijoux indiscrets* ("Sæpe turgentem spumantemque admovit oripriapum, simulque appressis ad labia labiis, fellatrice me linguā perfricuit...").

There could be an art of writing based on an interplay between the predictable and the unpredictable, between expectation and its disappointment, between collusion and surprise. Examples of such an art would be when exquisitely honed fine writing is dotted, as it were carelessly, with subtly trivial or slang expressions (Claudel, Lacan...); or the metamorphoses of Bolucra's name, in Raymond Queneau's

The Sunday of Life: Boulingra, Brelugat, Brolugat, Botugat, Botrulat, Brodugat, Bretoga, Butaga, Brelogat, Bretouilla, Bodrugat, etc.*

There could be an art of reading – and not just of reading written text, but also of what is called the reading of a painting, or a city – based on reading obliquely, on looking at the text from a different angle (but I have already abandoned the physiological level of reading: how could you teach your extra-ocular muscles to "read otherwise"?)

Voice, lips

It is considered vulgar to move your lips when reading. We were taught to read by being made to read aloud. Then we had to unlearn what we were told was a bad habit, presumably because it is too suggestive of application and effort.

That does not alter the fact that when we read our crico-arytenoid and cricothyroid muscles (which stretch and contract the vocal cords and the glottis) are active.

Reading is inseparable from lip-movement and vocal activity (there are texts which should only ever be mumbled or whispered, others you ought to be able to shout or hammer out).

---

* Two quotations seem to me appropriate to clarify this point and to broaden its import. First, Roger Price, in *In One Head and Out the Other* (Simon & Schuster, 1951): "A purged book (not to be confused with an expurgated or even with an unexpurgated book) is one in which the editor has *pencilled in* additional obscenities"; the second is the opening sentence of Roland Barthes's *Writing Degree Zero*: "Hébert never began an issue of *Le Père Duchêne* without first sprinkling a few "fucks" and "buggers" around the page. These obscenities meant nothing, but signified a great deal".

Hands

Not only the blind have trouble reading. The one-armed also have problems: they cannot turn the pages.
Hands are now used only for turning pages. The spread of the fully guillotined book has robbed today's reader of two great pleasures – the pleasure of cutting the pages (if I were Laurence Sterne I would now insert an entire chapter in praise of paper-knives, ranging from the humble cardboard cutter given away by booksellers to every purchaser of a book, to bamboo, polished stone, and steel paper-knives, not forgetting the scimitar designs (Tunisia, Algeria, Morocco), the matador-sword paper-knife (from Spain), the samurai-style cleaver (Japan) or those ghastly things in imitation-style leather sheaths which together with diverse other objects of the same ilk (scissors, pen-holder, pencil-box, universal calendar, memo pad, leather-clad integral desk-blotter, etc.) constitute what is known as a "desk set"); and the even greater pleasure of beginning to read a book with uncut pages. You will recall (for it wasn't that long ago, really) that books were made of signatures folded in such a way that the cuts needed alternated thus: eight pages needing, first, the upper edges cut and then, in two pairs, the side edges. The first eight pages could be read almost entirely without a paper-knife; of the next eight you could obviously read the first and last, and, by lifting them up, the fourth and fifth. But nothing more. The text came with gaps which held surprises and aroused expectations.

Posture

Reading posture is obviously too closely dependent on the environmental circumstances of the act, which I shall consider shortly, to be treated in its own right. Nonetheless it would be a fascinating area to research, as it is intrinsically connected to the sociology of the body, which, quite surprisingly, no sociologist or anthropologist has ever undertaken, despite the proposal of Marcel Mauss to which I referred at the beginning of this article. In the absence of any systematic study, all I can do is to offer a summary listing:

reading standing up (it's the best way of using a dictionary)

reading sitting down, but there are so many ways of being seated: feet on the ground, feet higher than the seat, the body stretched back (armchair, divan), elbows resting on a table, etc.

reading lying down: supine, prone, lying on the side, etc.

reading whilst kneeling (children leafing through a picture book; Japanese?)

reading squatting (Marcel Mausss, op. cit. p. 107: "The squatting position, in my opinion, is an interesting posture that could be retained from childhood. It is a very stupid mistake to prevent children from squatting. All humankind, excepting only our societies, has retained it.")

reading while walking. You think first of the priest reading his prayer book whilst taking his constitutional. But there are also tourists wandering through a foreign city with a map in their hand, or moving from one picture to another in a gallery while reading the descriptions of them given in the guidebook. Or there's walking in the country reading aloud from a book held in your hand. It seems to me that has become less frequent.

II. Environment

I have always been the sort of person who enjoys reading. When I have nothing else to do, I read.
CHARLIE BROWN

Very crudely, two types of reading may be distinguished: reading accompanied by some other (active or passive) occupation, and reading accompanied only by itself. The first type would be appropriate to a gentleman leafing through a magazine while waiting his turn at the dentist's; the second would be appropriate to the selfsame gentleman once he had returned home, at peace with his ivories, and sat down at his desk to read *Memoirs of a Chinese Embassy* by Marquis de Mogès.

So you may read for the sake of reading, and reading may be the sole activity of some instant. Examples are provided by readers seated in the reading room of a library; as it happens, in fact, a library is the special place set aside for reading, one of the few places where reading is a collective activity (reading is not necessarily solitary, but it is usually an individual occupation; sometimes people read in pairs, forehead to forehead, or over each other's shoulder; or else you may reread aloud for the benefit of others; but the idea of several people simultaneously reading the same thing is rather astounding: perhaps gentleman in a club, reading *The Times*; or a group of Chinese peasants reading *The Little Red Book*).

A different example seems to me to be particularly well

illustrated by a photograph published some years ago in *L'Express* alongside a survey of French publishing: it depicted Maurice Nadeau ensconced in a comfortable armchair, surrounded by piles of books taller than he was.

Or again, a child reading or trying to read the chapter on natural history on which he fears he will be tested the next day.

It would not be hard to give more examples. What seems to me to link them is that in all these cases "reading for reading's sake" is connected to some kind of study, to something which is of the order of work or trade, in any case of the order of necessity. It would be necessary to be more precise, obviously, and in particular to find more or less satisfactory criteria for distinguishing work from non-work. In current circumstances it seems relevant to point out this difference: on the one hand, what might be called professional reading, to which you have to devote yourself entirely, to make it the sole object of an hour or a day; on the other hand, what we can call leisure reading, which is always accompanied by another activity.

This is what strikes me the most, as far as the present matter is concerned, in reading manners: not that reading is considered a leisure activity, but that, in general, it can never exist on its own; it has to be inserted into another necessity; it has to have a supporting activity: reading is associated with the idea of time to fill, lost time to be put to use by reading. Maybe the supporting activity is but a pretext for reading, but how do you know? Is a man reading on the beach on the beach to read, or is he reading because he is on the beach? Does Tristram Shandy's fragile destiny matter more to him than the sunburn he's getting on his calves? In any case, is it not right to question reading's environments? For reading is not just reading a text, decoding signs, ploughing through lines, exploring pages, traversing meanings; it is not just the abstract communion of author and reader, the mystical wedding of the idea and the Ear. It is also and simultaneously the noise of the metro, or the swaying of a railway carriage, or the heat of the sun on a beach and the shouting of the children playing further along, or the feeling of hot water in the bathtub, or the expectancy of sleep...

One example will allow me to make clearer the sense of this questioning (which you are perfectly entitled to consider otiose): a good ten years ago I was dining with a few friends in a not very grand restaurant (hors d'œuvre, dish of the day, cheese or dessert); at another table an already deservedly celebrated philosopher was dining; he was dining alone, and as he ate he read a cyclostyled tome which was probably a thesis. He read between each dish, and frequently between each mouthful, and we wondered, my friends and I, what the effect of this double activity might be, we wondered how the two things blended, what taste the words had, what meaning there might be in the cheese: mouthful, concept, mouthful, concept... How do you chew a concept? And how could you give an account of the effect of this twin nourishment, how could you describe or measure it?

The following enumeration is a sketch of a typology of reading situations. It has not been done for the sole pleasure of making lists, for it seems to me that it can serve as a starting point for a global description of urban activities in today's world. In the tangled web of daily rhythms there are, in all sorts of places, temporal nooks, crannies, and shelves for reading; as if reading, expelled from our lives by full timetables, but remembering those childhood days when we spent Thursday afternoons* flat on our bedspreads together with the three musketeers or the children of Captain Grant, as if reading were sneaking back into the gaps and fissures of our adult lives.

Waiting times

Acts of reading can be categorized by the time allotted to them. First come waiting times. You read whilst waiting at the barber's, at the dentist's (acts of reading undermined by apprehension); in the cinema queue, you read the programme; in official buildings (social security, post office, lost property office, etc.), while waiting for your number to come up.

Those with foresight who know that they will be queuing for a long time at the entrance to a stadium or an opera house equip themselves with a folding stool and a book.

The Body

Acts of reading can be classified by accompanying bodily functions:

Feeding: Reading whilst eating (see above). Examples: opening the mail, unfolding the newspaper at breakfast.

Grooming: Reading in the bath is held by some to be the supreme pleasure. However, the idea is often more agreeable than the reality. Most tubs turn out to be inconvenient

---

* In the 1950s there were no classes at school on Thursday afternoons. (Translator's note)

and short of special equipment – bookstand, floating cushion and easily accessible faucets and towels – and special precautions, it is no easier to read in the bath than to smoke a cigarette, for example. This is a minor problem of everyday life that designers ought to be thinking about.

Natural functions: Louis XIV held audience seated on his commode. It was quite unexceptional in the period. Our societies have become much more discreet (cf. *The Phantom of Liberty*). Notwithstanding, the toilet is a major site of reading. A profound relationship exists between relieving one's innards and reading the text: intense openness, heightened receptivity, a joy of reading. This meeting-point of gut and feeling is best described by James Joyce:

> Asquat on the cuckstool he folded out his paper turning its pages over on his bared knees. Something new and easy. No great hurry. Keep it a bit. Our prize titbit. Matcham's Masterstoke. Written by Mr. Philip Beaufoy. Playgoer's club, London. Payment at the rate of one guinea a column has been made to the writer. Three and a half. Three pounds three. Three pounds thirteen and six.
>
> Quietly he read, restraining himself, the first column and, yielding but resisting, began the second. Midway, his last resistance yielding, allowed his bowels to ease themselves quietly as he read, reading still patiently, that slight constipation of yesterday quite gone. Hope it's not too big bring on piles again. No, just right. So. Ah! Costive one tabloid of cascara sagrada. Life might be so. (*Ulysses*)

Sleeping: People read a lot before going to sleep, often in order to get to sleep, and they read even more when sleep doesn't come. As a weekend guest in someone's home, it is a great pleasure to come across books you have never read but have wanted to, or familiar books you haven't read for years. You carry off a dozen to your bedroom and read or reread them almost until dawn.

Social Spaces

Reading is rarely done at work, except when your work consists of reading.

Mothers read on park benches while watching their children at play.

Idlers browse at open-air second-hand bookstalls, or read the daily newspapers displayed in the windows of newspaper offices.

Drinkers read the evening papers as they sip aperitifs on café terraces.

Public transport

Reading is much performed on the way to and from work. Acts of reading could be classified by the mode of transport: cars and coaches are useless (reading gives you a headache); buses are better suited, but bus readers are rarer than you would think, no doubt because of what you can see on the streets.

The place for reading is the metro. That could almost be a definition. I continue to be amazed that neither the Minister of Culture nor the Secretary of State for Higher Education has ever exclaimed: "Honourable members should cease forthwith their demands for more money for libraries. The people's true library is the underground!" (thunderous applause from the government benches).

The metro has two advantages from the point of view of reading. The first is that a metro journey takes an almost perfectly precise amount of time (roughly ninety seconds between any two adjacent stops), thus allowing you to time your reading passage – two pages, five pages, or a whole chapter, according to the length of your journey. The second advantage is the twice-daily and five-times weekly recurrence of the same journey. A book begun on Monday morning will be finished on Friday evening...

Travel

You read a lot when you travel. There is even a special kind of literature – called station bookstall literature – provided for it. People read especially on trains. In aeroplanes, people tend to glance at magazines. Ships are rarer and rarer. From the point of view of reading, moreover, a ship is no more than a deckchair (see below).

Miscellaneous

Reading on holiday. Holiday reading. Reading for tourists. Reading for purists.

Reading when ill at home, at hospital, in convalescence. Etc.

I have paid no attention to what is being read – it could be a book, a newspaper, or a flier – only to the fact of reading, in different places, at different times. What happens to the text?

What remains of it? How is a novel lasting from Montgallet metro stop to Jacques-Bonsergent perceived? What in fact happens when a text is chopped up, when its appropriation is interrupted by a body, by other people, by time, by the hubbub of collective life? These are the questions I am asking, and I don't think it is a waste of a writer's time to ask himself these kinds of questions.

1976

ON THE DIFFICULTY OF
IMAGINING THE GOOD LIFE

I'd not like to live with Andress (Ursula), but sometimes I
would

I'd not like to live in a bar, but sometimes I would

I'd not like to live in a coral reef, but sometimes I would

I'd not like to live in a dungeon, but sometimes I wish I did

I'd not like to live in the East, but sometime I would

I like living in France, but sometimes I don't

I'd not like to live in Guernsey, but sometimes I would

I'd not like to live hand-to-mouth, but sometimes I would

I'd quite like to live on the ice cap, but not for too long

I'd not like to live on a junk, but sometimes I would

I'd not like to live in a kraal, but sometimes I would

I'd quite like to live on the Left Bank, but not always

I'd have quite liked to go to the moon, but it's a bit late now

I'd not like to live in a nunnery, but sometimes I would

I'd like to live to be old, but sometimes I wouldn't

I quite like living in Paris, but sometimes I don't

I'd not like living in Quebec, but sometimes I wish I did

I'd not like to live rough, but sometimes I wish I did

I'd not like to live on a submarine, but sometimes I would

I'd not like to live in a tower, but sometimes I would

I'd not like to live in the United States, though sometimes I
   wish I did

I'd not like to live in a village, but sometimes I would

I'd not like to live in a wigwam, but sometimes I would

I'd quite like to live in Xanadu, but not forever

I'd not like to live in Yorkshire, but sometimes I would

I'd not like us all to live in Zanzibar, but sometimes I would

1981

ON SPECTACLES

⊞ ON THE DIFFICULTY *of the topic in general and on my own difficulty in particular.* At first sight, if I may be so bold as to use that expression, spectacles are hardly conducive to flights of lyrical fancy, and seem to offer an arid and austere subject for an essay once one has observed that the emergence of these cunningly curved lenses marked a great step forward for mankind by permitting the poorly-sighted to see rather better, or less poorly, one has apparently said it all, apart from making elegant allusions to the fabulous achievements of men who, in the absence of spectacles, would never have been the men they were, such as Pope Leo X and Goya, Chardin, Theodore Roosevelt and Toulouse-Lautrec, not forgetting Gustav Mahler, Émile Littré the lexicographer, or Harold Lloyd.

Moreover, and this second point is no doubt of more weight than the first, it may well be the case that the topic is one on which I must perforce declare myself to be lacking in competence, purchase and insight. For being up to the present time gifted with adequate if not truly piercing eyesight, I have in fact never worn spectacles, and my knowledge of the topic is for this reason extremely limited, not to say non-existent. Innumerable philosophers and men of ideas have no doubt held forth with brilliance on subjects of which they had no knowledge, to begin with at least, but all the same, to ask a man who has never donned a pair of specs to write an essay on glasses seems to me, on the face of it, to be as dubious as asking for an essay on China from someone who has never been to China, for an essay on tricycles or Formula 1 racing cars from a double-decker-bus driver, for an encomium of beef steak from a vegetarian (the last example being rather badly chosen, since the vegetarian in question may detest red meat, while I have nothing against spectacles, personally).

⌗ *On the serenity I feel nonetheless on tackling the subject.* That said, it is with a warm feeling of benevolent neutrality that I offer the reader the following considerations. A be-spectacled writer might be tempted to speak for himself, to get carried away, to cross his own tracks and to loose the thread in unnecessary digressions and irrelevant details, he would show how all his miseries and all his joys sprang from the inadequate curvature of his cornea or of his crys-talline lens, and would obviously end up forgetting where he had put his glasses. Whereas I am able to consider the mat-ter dispassionately, without prejudice, with unblurred eyes, indifferent as to the rival claims of hypermetropic and my-opic vision, which I shall examine with clear-sighted detach-ment but not without both sympathy and conscientiousness.

⌗ *On my experience of glasses.* Though unspectacled, as I have already said, and will no doubt need to say again, I have at home several objects related not to the correction of sight, but to its protection, enhancement and even its subversion.

Namely: 1) protective devices *a*) a pair of heavy, round glasses with frames "made in France" of some material vaguely imitating tortoiseshell, which don't fit me at all and don't belong to me and *b*) a pair of skiing goggles composed of a kind of rubber mounting, an elastic head-band and a piece of yellow-orange translucent plastic fixed to the mounting by two press-studs, so it can be replaced, depending on the luminosity of the sky and snow, by one of two other pieces of plastic of different shades, both now lost; I used these goggles for two days five years ago and I will probably never use them again; I came across them more or less by chance when I opened a drawer; 2) augmenting devices *a*) a tiny pair of black metal opera glasses, giving only a poor degree of enlargement but quite handy, and as good at shrinking things as at enlarging them; I borrowed them a few years ago for a performance of *La Bohème* at the Paris Opera (with, unless I am mistaken, Pavarotti and Mirella Freni) and up to now I have omitted returning them to their rightful owner; *b*) three magnifying glasses: a jeweler's monocular magnifying glass, a rectangular steel-rimmed magnifying glass equipped with an oblique black plastic handle, and a large round magnifying glass with a Britannia-metal rim, a horn handle and two finely-worked ferrules; I like this glass so much that I had it put on the cover of one of my stories ("A Gallery Portrait"), which deals with the most meticulous description possible of a painting (in a general sort of way, I like magnifying glasses: I used to have a fourth, a brass or cast-iron-rimmed weaver's glass, but I have unfortunately mislaid it); 3) the subverting devices, finally, include a pair of joke spectacles whose "glasses" are two caricatures of eyes drawn on a special kind of paper, which it would be proper to call birefringent since it possesses the particular property of allowing you to see either a half-closed eye or a large, rather bleary, heavily cross-eyed wide-open eye, depending on how you incline your head; two tiny holes allow the wearer to watch the intolerable exasperation the spectacles immediately inspire in the person facing you.

⊞ *On what transpires when I don a pair of spectacles.* In a one-off and frankly experimental way I do also have a pair of real glasses. I borrowed them from a friend who has a dozen pairs, big ones, small ones, oval and square pairs, round ones, clear and tinted ones, ones with an arm or a lens missing, etc. By putting them on I wished to verify a hypothesis that no optician would accept unreservedly, but which seems inherently probable to me, namely that what I can see with these glasses on resembles what is seen by a person who really needs them when he has taken them off. I don't know if I am making my meaning clear, but the effect, at any rate, is quite startling. The experiment takes only two or three minutes to give me a fairly dreadful headache, but in those minutes I experience a whole range of impressions each more bewildering than the last. If I look at something very close up (for instance, by leaning over the paper on which I am writing these lines) I feel I am seeing much better, with unprecedentedly sharp relief, a little like the feeling you have when you use that instrument of recreational physics which used to be called a stereoscope; if I raise my head and look around me slowly, everything goes fuzzy, wobbly, slightly clouded: things buckle at the edges, perspective goes flat, details become confused, and the slightest movement of my head makes it seem as though what I can see is moving with me, as if space had become unstable and even, to be honest, a little viscous; but if I should have the misfortune to stand up, to look at my feet or to walk a few steps, then, it seems to me, all the suffering of the poorly sighted is painfully revealed: my feet are so far away that I begin to wonder how they manage to carry me and to obey my commands, the floor moves, the walls pitch and toss. Roughly, I reckon, what Fernandel must have felt (in a film called, I think, *Public Enemy Number One*, unless it was *The Man in the Raincoat*) when, on waking, bat-blind and squinting, he fumbles along a thick black stripe leading from his bed to his bathroom shelf where, tidy man that he was, he had put his glasses away before he went to bed. It's a classic example of the kind of gag that delights me, and all the more so because it is completely pointless, as common sense would have prompted Fernandel to put his specs away in his bedside table. Or what Raymond Queneau's Pierrot might have felt when, as the sidekick of Crouïa-Bey, wearing a Persian costume but keeping his eyes down, he manages to grasp after a long and painful adjustment of his vision, what exactly the said fakir does with the hatpins he hands him.

⊞ *On the history of the world before spectacles.* Classical painting offers countless examples of people depicted while reading or writing. For instance, listed in no order, Antonello da Messina's *Virgin of the Annunciation*, at the Munich Pina-kothek; Rubens's portrait of Paracelsus, in Brussels; also in Brussels, Van Orley's portrait of the doctor Georges de Zelle; Rubens's portrait of Christophe Plantin, at the Plantin-Moretus Museum in Antwerp; Hans Holbein the Younger's portrait of Erasmus, in Basel, and the one by Quentin Metsys, in Rome; Rogier van der Weyden's Saint Yves, in London; Rembrandt's mother, by Gerard Dou, in Rotterdam; the portrait of a gentleman by Lorenzo Lotto, in Venice; the young girl reading a letter, by Jean Raoux, at the Louvre; the prophet Jeremiah, by the master of the Annunciation of Aix-en-Provence, in Brussels; the portrait of Jonathan Swift by Charles Gervas, at the National Portrait Gallery, London; *Saint Jerome in his Study* by Antonello da Messina, in the National Gallery, London; or Carpaccio's Saint Augustine, in the Scuola di S. Giorgio degli Schiavoni, in Venice. Quite frequently the individuals portrayed raise their heads to pose and look upwards or diagonally. But it is interesting to look at those who go on reading. The prophet Jeremiah seems to have perfectly normal sight; so does Jean Raoux's girl, though she has to lean heavily to catch a source of light; Saint Yves is pretty short-sighted and Rembrandt's mother utterly so; Saint Jerome, for his part, is clearly long-sighted.

How did people manage before glasses existed? You can ask this sort of question about dozens of other items or everyday life (erasers, scissors, scales, watches, compasses, magnets, mattresses, irons, latches, wheels, braces, toothbrushes, and pasta, which was brought back to us in 1295, from China, as everyone knows, by Marco Polo). The only possible answer is: people managed without, or they didn't manage, which is to say, in the present context, that they screwed up their eyes, pored over things, and got their noses wet when they drank their soup. Perhaps they drank infusions of hawkweed, so named because it was good for hawk's eyes, but that's hardly likely.

⊞ *On the invention of spectacles.* The invention of eyeglasses has been variously attributed to: *a*) the Chinese (of course); *b*) the Arab physician Ibn al-Haytham al-Hazîn (Abû 'Ali Muhammed ibn al-Hasan, also known as Alhaçan), Al-Hazem, whose cognomen was Ptolemæus Secundus, born

Basra 965 c.e., died Cairo 1039 c.e.; c) to Roger Bacon (1214–1294), also known as the "Admirable Doctor", who is also said to have invented the air-pump, gunpowder, and a plan to reform the calendar; d) to the Florentine physicist Salvino degli Armati (1245–1317), whose work on the power and the refraction of light weakened his sight while he was still young; seeking to remedy his infirmity, he discovered, around 1280, two glasses which, at particular degrees of curvature and thickness, magnified objects. He was thus the inventor of spectacles and wanted to keep the secret (I wonder why?); but his friend Alessandro della Spina, a Dominican friar from the monastery of Santa Caterina at Pisa, gave it away (Dézobry and Bachelet, *Dictionnaire de biographie*); e) to Alessandro della Spina (see above); f) and even to the Neapolitan J. B. Porta (1540–1615), also alleged to be the inventor of the camera obscura and the author of fourteen comedies, two tragedies and one tragi-comedy.

That makes a lot of people. And I have simplified the story quite considerably, for convex glasses (for hypermetropia) were invented well before concave lenses (for myopia).

⊞ *On the past diversity of spectacles.* There are not only spectacles, or rather there used to be not only spectacles: there were also single and double eyeglasses, hand-glasses, lorgnettes, pebbles and preserves. Hard to sort it all out. The draft classification which follows is based on three criteria: the number of lenses, the nature of the lenses, and the presence or absence of arms.

1.1   One lens, no arms: monocle

1.2   One lens, with arms: Cyclops's spectacle (rare)

2.1 Two lenses without arms

2.1.1 Hand-held: lorgnette

2.1.2 Supported by the bridge of the nose: pince-nez, or eyeglasses. (The two terms are supposed to be synonymous; but for pince-nez alone, Larive & Fleury's *Dictionary of Words and Things* (vol. 2, p. 417) distinguishes the ordinary pince-nez, the Japanese pince-nez, the clawed pince-nez, the adjustable pince-nez and the fitz-u.)

2.2 Two lenses with arms

2.2.1 With refracting lenses: spectacles in the proper sense (in fact there are several kinds of arms – temporal, split, etc., but that would take us too far).

2.2.2 Preserves, sometimes with smoked glass, are presbyopic spectacles that dare not speak their name.

I hope things are clearer now.

⊞ *On spectacles today.* Lorgnettes, pince-nez, monocles, eyeglasses and preserves are nowadays no more than period props for films set in the Belle Époque. On the other hand, we have a great number of contemporary glasses for special purposes; gangers' or stonemasons' glasses (which are in fact eyeshields, having, in place of lenses, pieces of fine metallic mesh), engineering goggles, welders' eyeshields (the real heroes, at least on the posters, of the film *The Confession*), motorcyclists' glasses, skiing goggles, diving goggles, mountaineering goggles, etc., not forgetting all the varieties of sunglasses.

⊞ *On frames.* A frame consists of two circles, a bridge, and two arms. The shape of the bridge varies according to the shape of the nose which it has to fit. At the end of the last century, distinctions were made between:

- the X-bridge for flat noses
- the K-bridge for convex noses
- the C-bridge for very prominent noses

This information was gleaned from the irreplaceable Larive & Fleury, which also specifies that the best frames are made of steel, which retains its shape, that silver and gold are only used for ostentation, and that buff and tortoise-shell acquire a dirty and disagreeable colour with age.

⊞ *On living with spectacles.* There would be a lot to say about the way people live with their glasses, about the way they turn into gestures, habits, and codes the deficiency, the fuzziness which one day obliged them to correct the inadequacies of their eyes by the use of these portable prostheses. One day they found they had a pair of glasses, and a whole series of gestures became theirs, began to become part of their everyday lives, and to mark them out as clearly as the way they spoke, the way they folded their napkin or read their newspaper. We should consider those gestures, performed many dozens of times a day: the way they settle their glasses on the bridge of their nose, the way they remove them, the way they put them away, their ways of cleaning them and handling them. In short, we ought to do for glasses the kind of work Marcel Mauss proposed for what he called "body techniques", an attempt to describe and compare the ways people eat, sleep, wash, use tools (for example, during the 1914–1918 war, English soldiers were given French spades, but didn't know what to do with them, which obliged the quartermaster general's department to substitute 8,000 spades (English) for 8,000 spades (French), and vice versa, every time a division from the one country came up to the front to relieve a division of the other), walk, dance, jump, etc.*

Unfortunately I have not had the time to collect sufficient information to render such a study purposeful or worthwhile. I would have had to live in the company of the bespectacled for at least a few days, noting down carefully everything they did with their glasses. I can offer at most a few elementary and obvious observations.

⊞ *Specificity of use.* Some wearers wear their glasses all day long, others only in well-defined circumstances – for driving, for instance, or for reading. One of my friends noticed during a stay in Venice that he couldn't manage to read the really small print in his guide-book when visiting the churches, so he had a pair of half-moon spectacles made which allowed him to read when he lowered his eyes and to see the paintings when he raised them.

⊞ *Where spectacles are kept.* Some people keep their glasses on even when not using them; they push them up onto their forehead or even into their hair; others, no doubt forever fearful of losing their glasses, have them hang around their neck on a string or chain; yet others put them away carefully in a specially-designed case; then there are those who need two pairs of glasses, one for long distance, the other for near sight, and who spend their time changing from one

---

* Marcel Mauss, *Sociology and Psychology*, trans. Ben Brewster. London: Routledge, 1979, p. 99.

pair to the other; yet others seem to have always forgotten where they have put their specs and rush around the house shouting "Where did I put my glasses?"; and still others will always put them away strictly in the same place, in a drawer, on the bathroom shelf, or next to the television.

⊞ *Wiping.* I can shed little light on this matter; I know there is a special tissue given away free by some opticians to every buyer of a pair of spectacles, or even just a frame. Many people, on the other hand, seem to use whatever comes to hand when the need to wipe their glasses comes upon them: a handkerchief, a Kleenex, a napkin, the corner of the tablecloth, or the end of a tie, etc.

⊞ *Gestures with glasses.* As spectacles are supposed to give the wearer a sterner look, some people take them off as a sign of warmth; I remember seeing examiners do that to reassure candidates quaking at the idea of having to speak on the four-field farming system or on the colonization of Dahomey by General Dodds; rubbing your forehead with your glasses, or chewing the ends of the arms are signs of deep thought.

⊞ *On Fashion.* Most objects and accessories of everyday life are liable to being marked out, singularized and endowed with extra value by the signature – the French call it the "paw" – of a prestigious designer.

Spectacles, no more than pens, cigarette-lighters, hand-bags, suitcases, key wallets, shoes, gloves, cigarette-cases, ties, watches, and cufflinks, have not escaped the brush of luxury, the real end of which remains obscure to me.

⊞ *On advertising.* Advertising used to praise the virtues of the lenses: glasses were made to see better with. I remember the last three lines of an advertising jingle which I used to see for years in the shop-window of an optician in Rue de Passy. The poster depicted an old lady smiling and the text went like this:

> *Les rides sur son front ont tracé leurs sillons*
> *Mais ses yeux sont gardés des atteintes de l'âge*
> *Grâce aux verres STIGMAL aux lunettes HORIZON*

> Though her brow may be wrinkled and wizened
> Her sight has not been affected by age
> Thanks to lenses by STIGMAL in frames
>   by HORIZON

I also remember a poster depicting a woman's face encased in a rather alarming helmet that was meant to test her eyesight (and another sinister memory of the advertising slogan used under the Occupation by a famous optician to make it clear that his name, despite its sound, was absolutely not Jewish).

Today, as far as fashion and the marketplace are concerned, glasses are made less to help you see than to be worn, and advertising focuses on the frames. Advertising captions for glasses are often puns: "Guess the price, just to see", or "This half's on spec" (advertising frames sold at fifty percent discount by what regular opticians in France call "outsiders").

⊞ *On language.* While French is almost as rich as English in expressions related to seeing (the wood for the trees, eye to eye, stars, the light of day, the end of the tunnel, to see black, to see it coming, to see it floating in the air, a sight for sore eyes, make eyes at, eyewash, eye-opener, eyeball to eyeball), metaphors, idioms and proverbs based on glasses are very rare and moreover almost all obsolete. Does anyone still say "a nose for spectacles" for "a big nose"? In seventeenth-century French, "to put your glasses on better" meant "to pay more heed", but I don't think anyone uses that expression any more. Saint-Simon once used the expression "to put glasses on" to mean "to give the appearance of severity", and Molière "she's for bespectacled eyes", meaning "she only likes intellectuals", but these images did not really pass into popular language. As for proverbs, "Every man sees through his own spectacles" (everyone has his own point of view), and *"Bonjour lunettes, adieu fillettes"*, translated by Lachatre as "when the time comes to wear spectacles, philandering has to be renounced". I think they are only ever found in the old dictionaries and almanacs where I looked them up.

⊞ *By way of conclusion.* There are a certain number of things that I know I shall almost certainly never do in the future. It is exceedingly unlikely I shall ever go to the moon, or travel by submarine, or learn Chinese, or the saxophone, or ergometry, even if sometimes I really would like to. It is also highly improbable that I should be one day an officer on active service, a docker at Valparaiso, a director of a major bank, a corner-shop keeper, a peasant, or a president of the Republic.

On the other hand it is almost certain that one day, in common, apparently, with one third of the French population, I shall wear glasses. My ciliary muscle, which controls the changes in the curvature of the crystalline lens, will lose its elasticity bit by bit and then my eye will no longer be able to adjust its focus. It happens to all adults from the age of forty-five. I'm forty-four and a half. . .

1980

THOUGHTS OF SORTS/
SORTS OF THOUGHTS

I) *Summary*

SUMMARY – Methods – Questions – Vocabulary exercises –
The world as a jigsaw – Utopias – Twenty thousand leagues
under the sea – Reason and thought – Eskimos – The Universal Exhibition – Alphabet – Classifications – Hierarchies
– My sorts – Borges and the Chinese – Sei Shônagon –
Ineffable joys of enumeration – Book of records – Lowness
and inferiority – The dictionary – Jean Tardieu – My
thoughts – On aphorisms – "In a network of lines that
intersect" – Miscellaneous – ?

N) *Methods*

Obviously, at different stages in this paper's development –
notes scrawled on pads or on loose sheets, transcribed quotations, "ideas", see, cf., etc. – I accumulated little lists, small
b, ROMAN I, thirdly, part two. Then when it came to bring-
ing these pieces together (and I had no choice but to bring
them together if this "paper" were ever to cease being just a

vague plan regularly postponed to a less busy future point in time) it quickly became obvious that I would never manage to organize them into a coherent language.

It was rather as if the images and ideas I had had, and however potentially scintillating they may have first seemed in isolation or even in opposing pairs, had distributed themselves around the imaginary space of my as-yet-unwritten pages like the noughts (or crosses) that a third-rate player had dotted around a grid, unable to get three to line up in a row (or column).

The deficiency of language is not due only to my laziness (or low standard of noughts and crosses); it has more to do with what I have tried to target, if not to hit upon, in the subject I have been given for this essay. It is as if the questioning prompted by the title, "Thoughts of Sorts / Sorts of Thoughts", questioned thinking and sorting in such a way as to make "thinking" unthinkable except in splinters, in dispersion, forever returning to the fragmentation it was supposed to try to put in order.

What hove into my mind's eye were things all fuzzy and wavering, fleeting and unfinished, and in the end I decided to retain the perplexed and uncertain character of these shapeless scraps, to stop short of pretending to organize them into anything that might have a claim to the appearance (and the charm) of an article with a beginning, a middle, and an end.

Maybe I have answered the question set before asking it. Maybe I have avoided asking it so as not to have to answer. Maybe I am using, and abusing, the old rhetorical figure called excuse, in which instead of tackling the problem to be solved you just answer questions with other questions and hide behind more or less feigned incompetence.

Maybe what I am doing is also saying that the question is unanswerable, that thinking refers ultimately to the unthinking underneath it, and that what's really filed away in well-sorted files, what they serve to mask, ferociously, is the unsortable, the unnameable, and the unsayable. . .

A) *Questions*

THOUGHTS / SORTS

What does the forward-slash mean?

What exactly is the question? Whether I think before I sort? Whether I sort before I think? How do I sort out my thoughts? What thoughts do I have when I want to sort them out?

E) *Vocabulary exercises*

Sort the following verbs into the right order: catalogue, categorise, classify, collect, enumerate, file, group, list, number, order, rank, shelve, sort, subdivide.

They are given in alphabetical order.

These verbs cannot all be synonyms of each other: why would we need fourteen verbs to describe the same action? *Ergo*, they are different. But how are they different? Some pair off into natural opposites around a common preoccupation, for example, dividing summons up the idea of a set to the distributed into different subsets, and grouping, which suggests separate subsets being brought together into a single set.

Others suggest yet more terms (for example: distribute, discriminate, characterize, mark, define, distinguish, oppose, etc.) taking us back to the primal babble that speaks obscurely of what we might call the readable (what our mental faculties can read, apprehend, or understand).

T) *The World as a Jigsaw*

> *Plants are divided into trees, flowers, and vegetables.*
> Stephen Leacock

It's so tempting to try to sort out the whole world by a single code; to find a universal law ruling over all phenomena; two hemispheres, five continents, masculine and feminine, animal and vegetable, singular and plural, left and right, four seasons, five senses, six vowels, seven days, twelve months, twenty-six letters.

Unfortunately it doesn't work, it's never even had the slightest hope of working, it will never work.

That won't prevent people carrying on for many more years trying to categorize this or that animal according to whether it has an even number of toes or hollow horns.

W) *Utopias*

All utopias are depressing, because they leave no place for chance, for difference, for the miscellaneous. It's all been sorted into an order, and order reigns.

Lurking behind every utopia is a great taxonomic design: a place for everything and every thing in its place.

O) *Twenty Thousand Leagues Under the Sea*

Conseil knows how to TAG fish.
Ned Land knows how to NAB fish.
Conseil sorts into batches the fish Ned Land catches.

R) *Reason and Thought*

What is the relationship, in fact, between reason and thought (independently of the fact that the two words served as the titles of two philosophy journals)? Dictionaries do not give much help with an answer; for example, in *Collins English Dictionary* THOUGHT = the act or process of thinking, and REASON = the faculty of rational argument; it seems to me more likely that we will discover a relationship or a difference between the two terms by studying the adjectives which may qualify them: thought may be touching, deep, banal, or free; reason may be deep too, but it can also be pure, good, valid, idle, opposite, woman's, untrammelled, sound, or of State.

K) *Eskimos*

Eskimos, so I have been told, have no *generic* term for ice, but several words (I have forgotten the exact number, but I think it is large, something like a dozen) referring to various specific qualities of water between its entirely liquid state and the forms it takes when frozen more or less hard.

It is obviously difficult to find an equivalent example in French or English; perhaps Eskimos have only one word to refer to the space separating their igloos whereas we have, in French, at least seven (*rue, avenue, boulevard, place, cours, impasse, venelle*), and in English at least twenty (street, avenue, crescent, place, road, row, lane, mews, gardens, terrace, yard, square, circus, grove, court, greens, houses, gate, ground, way, drive, walk), but all the same we do have a word which includes them all (*artère*, thoroughfare). Similarly if we are talking to a pastry-cook about the cooking of sugar, he will reply most pertinently that he cannot grasp *exactly* what we mean unless we specify the amount of cooking required (to the pearl, until lumpy, until caramelized, etc.); nonetheless, the concept "cooking sugar" will be perfectly clear to him.

F) *The Universal Exhibition*

The objects exhibited at the Paris Exhibition of 1900 were divided into eighteen groups and 121 classes. "The products", wrote Monsieur Picard, chief commissioner of the Universal Exhibition, "must be presented to visitors in logical order, and the order must be based on simple, clear and definite concepts, containing their own philosophy and their own justification, so that the commanding idea is easily apparent".

On reading Monsieur Picard's programme, what is especially apparent is that the commanding idea was rather thin.

A weary metaphor justified the first place given to education and teaching: "This is where man *enters* life". Works of art come next because they have to keep "their place of honour". "Reasons of the same order" mean that "Instruments and general techniques of Arts and Letters" occupy the third place. In the sixteenth subclass, for reasons I cannot divine, you find medicine and surgery (straitjackets, sickbeds, crutches, and wooden legs, field surgeons' equipment, Red Cross rescue kits, resuscitation equipment for victims of drowning and suffocation, rubber goods made by the firm of Bognier and Burnet, etc.).

From the fourth to the fourteenth group, categories follow one after the other without any glimmer of a system emerging. You can just about grasp the succession of groups

four, five, and six (machinery; electricity; civil engineering
and transport), and of groups seven, eight, and nine (agri-
culture; horticulture and arboriculture; forestry, hunting
and fishing) but after that things are all over the place:

Group 10: Food

Group 11: Mines and metallurgy

Group 12: Decoration and furnishings of public buildings and dwelling houses

Group 13: Fibres, fabrics, clothing

Group 14: Chemical industry

The fifteenth group is devoted, as it had to be, to everything that hasn't got a place in the other fourteen, that is to
say to "miscellaneous industries" (stationery; cutlery; jew-
ellery; watchmaking; bronze, cast, and wrought ironwork,
embossed metals; brushware, leatherware, fancy goods and
wickerwork; rubber and gutta-percha; toy trade).

The sixteenth group (labour welfare, including public
hygiene and poor relief) is where it is because it (the welfare
of labour) "had to come *naturally* (the italics are mine) in the
wake of the various branches of artistic, agricultural and
industrial production [since] it is their result as well as their
philosophical basis".

The seventeenth group is devoted to "colonisation"; it is a
new group (compared to the 1889 Exhibition) whose "cre-
ation is amply justified by the need for colonial expansion
felt by all civilised nations".

The last place, finally, is taken simply by the army and
navy.

The allocation of products within these groups to their
classes holds innumerable surprises; but it is not possible to
go into those details here.

L) *The Alphabet*

I have wondered many times what logic rules the distribution of the six vowels* and twenty consonants in our alphabet. The obvious impossibility of answering that query is, to begin with, quite reassuring: alphabetical order is arbitrary, non-expressive, and thus, neutral; objectively, A is worth no more than B, ABC is not a sign of excellence, but just of a beginning (as easy as ABC).

But given an order, any order, a qualitative value always sneaks in sooner or later, whether we like it or not, and gives meaning to the places of the elements in the order. That's why a "B" movie is considered "less good" than some other film which no-one, however, has ever thought of calling an "A" film; that's why a cigarette manufacturer who prints "Class A" on his packets means us to understand that his cigarettes are better than others.

The quality code of alphabetical order is not very rich; in fact, it has only three elements: A for excellent, B for less good and Z for rock bottom (in French, really rotten films can be called "Z movies").

But that doesn't stop it from being a code, nor from superimposing a hierarchy onto a sequence that is inert by definition.

For rather different reasons which are nonetheless adjacent to our subject, numerous firms and companies attempt to give themselves names which will result in acronyms of the type "AAA" or "ABC" or "AAAC", etc., so as to come at the head of the list in trade and telephone directories.

---

* In French, Y counts as a vowel.

On the other hand, a schoolboy has every interest in bearing a name with an initial somewhere in the middle of the alphabet as it gives him a greater chance of not being picked on to answer test questions.

S) *Classifications*

Taxonomic vertigo exists. I suffer it every time my eyes alight upon a list of Universal Decimal Classification (UDC, or Dewey Decimal) numbers. By what sequence of miracles was it ever agreed, more or less all over the world, that

$$668.184.2.099$$

refers to toilet soap (finishing processes), and

$$629.1.018\text{-}465$$

refers to ambulance sirens, whereas

$$621.3.027.23$$
$$621.436{:}384$$
$$616.24\text{-}002.5\text{-}084$$
$$796.54$$
$$913.15$$

refer respectively to electrical tension under fifty volts, foreign trade in diesel engines, prophylactics for tuberculosis, camping, and the historical geography of China and Japan!

H) *Hierarchies*

There are undergarments, garments, and overgarments, with no sense of hierarchy between them. But if there are secretaries and undersecretaries, underlings, undergraduates, and undersherriffs, there are almost never any oversecretaries or overlings; in French there's only one (obsolete) instance, *surintendant,* and in English we have no more than overlord and overseer; perhaps more significantly, in the civil service there are deputy undersecretaries and above them undersecretaries, but above the undersecretaries there are no oversecretaries or supersecretaries, but the big fish ominously called *permanent* secretaries.

Sometimes the underbody persists even when the overbody has changed its name: in the hierarchy of French libraries, there are no longer any librarians – they are called keepers and are allocated either to a scale point or to the rank of head keeper (scale 2, scale 1, special scale, head keeper); meanwhile, down below, sublibrarians plod on.

C) *How I sort*

My problem with sorting orders is that they do not last; I have scarcely finished filing things before the filing system is obsolete.

Sometimes I am seized, as I suppose everyone is, with a furious need to tidy things away. The sheer quantity of things to tidy, the near-impossibility of sorting them out by really satisfactory criteria, mean that I never get to the end of it, that I don't get beyond sorting into provisional and ill-defined categories, scarcely more efficient than the initial anarchy.

As a result I end up with really odd categories; for instance, a file full of miscellaneous papers inscribed with the words "To Be Sorted"; or a drawer labeled "Urgent 1" containing nothing (in the drawer marked "Urgent 2" are a few old photographs, and in "URGENT 3," spare exercise books).

Overall, I manage to cope.

Y) *Borges and the Chinese*

A) those that belong to the emperor, B) embalmed ones, C) those that are trained, D) suckling pigs, E) mermaids, F) fabulous ones, G) stray dogs, H) those that are included in this classification, I) those that tremble as if they were mad, J) innumerable ones, K) those drawn with a very fine camel's hair brush, L) others, M) those that have just broken a flower vase, N) those that resemble files from a distance.

Michel Foucault has popularized very widely this "classification" of animals that Jorge Luis Borges attributes, in *Other Inquisitions*, p. 103, to a Chinese encyclopædia which someone called Dr. Franz Kuhn is said to have once had in his hands. The multiplicity of intermediaries, as well as Borges's well-known taste for fake scholarship, allow us to wonder whether this almost too perfectly mind-boggling jumble is not primarily a piece of artistry. But just by dipping into a few official documents, an almost equally flabbergasting list can easily be produced:

A) animals on which bets are laid, B) animals which may not be hunted between 1 April and 15 September, C) beached whales, D) animals subject to quarantine on entry into France, E) animals in joint ownership, F) stuffed animals, G) et cetera*, H) animals which are carriers of leprosy,

---

* There's nothing intrinsically odd about "etc."; it's just its position in the list that makes it seem bizarre.

I) blind dogs, J) animals to which large estates have been bequeathed, K) animals which may be taken on board, L) lost dogs without collars, M) asses, N) mares thought to be gravid.

U) *Sei Shônagon*

Sei Shônagon does not sort; she lists, and begins again. One theme sets off one list, of things or of anecdotes. Later, an almost identical theme will produce a different list, and so on; you end up with series you can divide into groups; for example, things that make your heart beat faster, things you are in a hurry to see or hear, things that move you deeply, or, in the series of unpleasant "things":

> depressing things
> hateful things
> annoying things
> unsuitable things
> shameful things
> things that make you anxious
> people who seem to suffer
> unpleasant things
> things that are unpleasant to see

A dog howling in the daytime, a lying-in room when the baby has died, a cold, empty brazier, an ox-driver who hates his oxen, these come under depressing things; under hateful things, you find: a baby that starts crying just when one is about to be told some interesting piece of news, a flight of crows circling about with loud caws, and dogs when they bark for a long time in chorus; amongst people who seem to suffer: the nurse looking after a baby who cries at night; amongst things unpleasant to see: a high court noble's carriage that has dirty blinds.

D) *The Ineffable Joys of Enumeration*

There are two contradictory temptations in any act of enumeration: the first is to cover EVERYTHING, the second is to leave something out all the same; the first temptation would seek to close the question forever, the second would leave it open; between the exhaustive and the incomplete, enumeration seems to me to be, prior to any sort of thought (and prior to any thought of sorting), the intrinsic mark of our need to name and to collect without which the world ("life") would be unmappable: there are different things that are nonetheless a little bit the same; you can assemble them into series within which they can be further distinguished.

The notion that there is nothing in the world so unique that it cannot be put into some list or other is, to some degree, terrifying and intoxicating at the same time. Everything can be catalogued: editions of Tasso, Atlantic islands, the ingredients needed for a pear tart, the major relics, masculine nouns with feminine plurals (*amours*, *délices*, and *orgues*), Wimbledon finalists, or, arbitrarily restricted to ten elements:

1) Brû's brother-in-law's family name:

Bolucra
Bulocra
Brelugat

Brolugat
Botugat
Bodruga
Broduga
Bretoga
Butaga
Brétaga

2) hamlets near Palaiseau

Les Glaises
Le Pré-Poulin
La Fosse-aux-Prêtres
Les Trois-Arpents
Les Joncherettes
Les Clos
Le Parc-d'Ardenay
La Georgerie
Les Sablons
Les Plantes

3) the sufferings of Mr. Zachary McCaltex

made dizzy by the bouquet of 6,000 dozen roses
cuts his foot on an open tin
half-eaten by a wild cat
post-alcoholic paramnesia
overcome by sleep
nearly knocked down by a truck
brings up his meal
a five-month-old sty
insomnia
alopecia

B) *The Book of Records*

The preceding lists are not sorted alphabetically or chronologically or logically; today's misfortune is that most firms and television programmes have been ranked for a long time now solely in terms of their box-office (or hit parade) success; recently, the book magazine *Lire* even "sorted out thought" by holding a referendum to decide which intellectuals hold greatest sway.

If we have to list records, it would be better to find them in fields slightly more eccentric with respect to our main subject: Mr. David Maund owns 6,506 miniature bottles; Mr. Robert Kaufman has 7,495 kinds of cigarettes; Mr. Ronald Rose made a champagne cork pop a distance of thirty-one meters; Mr. Isao Tsychiya shaved 233 people in one hour, and Mr. Walter Cavanagh possesses 1,003 valid credit cards.

G) *Lowness and Inferiority*

What complex made two French departments, Seine-Inférieure and Charente-Inférieure, eager to lose their designations as "inferior" and become respectively Seine and Charente-*Maritime*? Similarly, the "Lower Pyrenees" have been redubbed "Atlantic Pyrenees", and the "Lower Alps" have become the "Alps of Upper Provence"; and Loire-Inférieure has turned itself into Loire-Atlantique. On the other hand, for reasons that escape me, the department of Bas-Rhin ("Low Rhine") has not taken offence at being the neighbour of Haut-Rhin ("High Rhine").

One may note that, in similar fashion, the departments of Marne, Savoie, and Vienne have never felt belittled by the existence of Haute-Marne, Haute-Savoie and Haute-Vienne, which must say something about the different roles of marked and unmarked terms in classifications and hierarchies.

V) *The Dictionary*

I own one of the oddest dictionaries in the world; it is entitled: *Manuel biographique ou Dictionnaire historique abrégé des grands hommes depuis les temps les plus reculés jusqu'à nos jours* ("Biographical handbook, or abridged historical dictionary of great men from the earliest times to the present"); it dates from 1825 and its publisher was none other than Roret, the publisher of a famous series of handbooks on arts and crafts.

The dictionary is in two parts and is 588 pages long in all; the first 288 pages are taken up by the first five letters of the alphabet; the second part (300 pages) is devoted to the other twenty-one letters. The first five letters get fifty-eight pages each on average, the last twenty-one get only fourteen; I certainly know that the frequency of the letters is far from uniform (in the *Larousse du XXe siècle*, A, B, C, and D take up two whole volumes out of six), but Roret's distribution is really far too unbalanced. If you compare it to the distribution of Lalanne's *Biographie universelle* (Dubochet, 1844), for example, you find that the letter C occupies proportionately three times as much space, A and E twice as much, but that M, R, S, T, and V get about half as much.

It would be interesting to look more closely at how this unfairness has affected the articles themselves: were they edited down, and if so, how? Were some of them simply cut, and if so which, and on what criteria? As a case in point,

Anthemius, a sixth-century architect to whom we owe (in part) Hagia Sophia, is entitled to a thirty-one-line article, whereas Vitruvius gets only six lines; Anne de Boulen or Boleyn also has thirty-one lines, but Henry VIII is only given nineteen.

H) *Jean Tardieu*

In the 1960s a device was invented which allows continuous variation of the focal distance of a movie-camera lens, thus simulating (fairly crudely) the effect of movement without the camera itself actually needing to be moved. The device is called a "zoom-lens" and the corresponding verb, "to zoom", though not yet acknowledged in dictionaries, quickly came into the language of the profession.

Such is not always the case: for example, most motor cars have three pedals and for two of them there is a specific verb: to accelerate and to brake. But there is no simple verb, as far as I know, for the third pedal: you have to say "to depress the clutch", "to bring the clutch in/out", etc. Similarly there are verbs for shoe-laces (to lace), buttons (to button) but in French there is none for zip-fasteners; neither English nor French has yet invented a verb for Velcro.

The English language also possesses a verb meaning "to live in the suburbs and work in town" (to commute), but like French it is bereft of a term meaning "to drink a glass of white wine with a mate from Burgundy at the Deux-Magots Café around six in the evening on a rainy day whilst discussing the meaning of life, realizing you have just met your old chemistry teacher and that a young woman next to you has just said to her companion, 'I gave him a right earful and a piece of my mind, believe you me!'" (Jean Tardieu, "Minor problems and practical exercises", *Un mot pour un autre*, NRF, 1951).

P) *How I think*

When I think, how do I think? How do I think when I am not thinking? In this precise instant, how do I think when I am thinking about how I think when I do think?

"Thinking/sorting", for instance, brings to my mind "drinking/sporting", or "ink-writ thing-song" or "sort of sinking". Is that's what's meant by thinking?

I am not often visited by thoughts about the infinitesimally small, or about Cleopatra's nose, or about where the holes in Emmenthaler come from, or about the Nietzschean sources of Agatha Christie or Joe Shuster; my thoughts are much more like doodles, internal memos, commonplaces.

But all the same, when thinking (musing?) about this essay ("Thoughts of Sorts / Sorts of Thoughts"), how did I come to think of noughts and crosses, Leacock, Jules Verne, Eskimos, the Universal Exhibition, the words for "road" in English, permanent secretaries, Sei Shônagon, Queneau, Anthemius, and Vitruvius? The answer to these questions is sometimes obvious and sometimes completely obscure: I could only talk in terms of fumbling, flair, hints, chance, fortuitous encounters, or intended connections, or fortuitously intended connections:

meandering among words: I don't think but look for my words: somewhere in the heap of words there must be one which will give shape to this vague, hesitating excitement, which later on, will "mean something".

It's also, and especially, a matter of *montage*, or distortions, contortions, detours, and reflecting mirrors
and of structures, as the following paragraph proposes to demonstrate.

X) *On Aphorisms*

Marcel Benabou (*Un Aphorisme peut en cacher un autre*, Bibliothèque Oulipienne, no. 13, 1980) has designed a machine for producing aphorisms. It consists of two parts; a grammar and a lexicon.

The grammar lists a certain number of structures often found in common-or-garden aphorisms, for instance:

Better to be *A* than *B*
He who *A*s last *A*s longest
A is the continuation of *B* by other means
One man's *A* is another man's *B*
Great *A*s from little *B*s do grow
*A*s wouldn't be *A*s if they weren't *B*s
A broadens the mind
Etc.

The lexicon is a list of pairs (or triplets, or quads) of words which may be false synonyms (love/friendship, sense/ sensibility), antonyms (life/death, happy/wise, past/present), phonetically similar words (love/dove, wife/strife), words connected by usage (crime/punishment, oak/acorn, stone/ moss, hammer/sickle, being/nothingness), etc.

The injection of the vocabulary from the lexicon into the grammatical structures produces a more or less infinite number of aphorisms at will, each more meaningful than the last. Forthwith and henceforth a computer program, written by Paul Braffort, will spew out on request a baker's dozen in a few seconds:

> Better be oak than acorn
> He who travels last travels longest
> Love is the continuation of strife by other means
> One man's stone is another man's poison
> Great boys from little lads do grow
> Geese wouldn't be geese if they weren't gander
> Moss broadens the mind

and so on. Where is the thought? In the structure? In the lexicon? In the operation which combines them?

J) *"In a network of lines that intersect"*

The alphabet used to "number" the different paragraphs of this text follows the order of appearance of the letters of the alphabet in the seventh story of *If on a Winter's Night a Traveler...* by Italo Calvino.

The title of this tale, rendered by William Weaver as "In a network of lines that intersect", contains the first fourteen letters of this alphabet, up to the letter C. The first line gets you to the twenty-first letter, M, the second line gives you nothing, the third P; the last four letters, X, J, Q, Z, are to be found in lines 13, 18, 61, and 95 respectively.

It will be easily deduced that his tale is not a lipogram; it will likewise be noted that only one of the letters (Z) occupies the same place in that alphabet as it does in the so-called normal one.

Q) *Miscellaneous*

Classification of interjections, from a (pretty poor) crossword dictionary (extracts):

	French	English
Expressing:		
admiration	EH	WOW
anger	BIGRE	DARN
scorn	BEUH	POOH
Used by a carter to go forward:	HUE	GEE-UP
Expressing:		
noise of a falling body	PATATRAS	SPLAT
noise made by a thing	CRIC, CRAC	CLUNK
noise of a fall	POUF	SPLOSH
The song of the Bacchantes	EVOHÉ	EVOE
To rouse hunting dogs	TAIAUT	TALLY-HO
Expressing:		
disappointment	BERNIQUE	OH DEAR
an oath	MORDIENNE	ZOUNDS
a Spanish oath	CARAMBA	CARAMBA
Henry IV's favourite oath	VENTRE-SAINT-GRIS	FIDDLESTICKS

disapproval	PARBLEU	BLESS MY SOUL
Used to chase		
a person away	OUST, OUSTE	SHOO

Z) ?

1982

SOURCES

Statement of Intent : "Notes sur ce que je cherche", *Le Figaro*, 8 December 1978, p. 28.

Some Uses of the Verb "To Live": "De Quelques Emplois du verbe habiter", in *Construire pour habiter*. Paris: L'Équerre-Plan, 1981, pp. 4–5.

Notes on the Objects to Be Found on My Desk: "Notes concernant les objets qui sont sur ma table de travail", *Les Nouvelles littéraires*, no. 2521, 26 February 1976, p. 17.

Three Bedrooms Remembered: "Trois chambres retrouvées", *Les Nouvelles littéraires* no. 2612, 24 November 1977, p. 20.

Brief Notes on the Art and Craft of Sorting Books: "Notes brèves sur l'art et la manière de ranger ses livres", *L'Humidité*, no. 25, Spring 1978, pp. 35–38.

Twelve Sidelong Glances: "Douze regards obliques", *Traverses* 3 (1976), pp. 44–48.

Backtracking: "Les lieux d'une ruse", *Cause commune*, no. 1, 1977, pp. 77–88.

I Remember Malet & Isaac: "Je me souviens de Malet & Isaac", *H-Histoire*, no. 1, March 1979, pp. 197–209.

81 Easy-Cook Recipes: "81 fiches-cuisine à l'usage des débutants", in *Manger*. Christian Besson, Catherine Weinzaepflen, editors. Liège: Yellow Now/Maison de la culture, 1980, pp. 97–109.

Reading: "Lire: esquisse socio-physiologique", *Esprit*, no. 453, January 1976, pp. 9–20.

On the Difficulty of Imagining the Good Life: "De la difficulté qu'il y a à imaginer une Cité idéale", *La Quinzaine littéraire*, no. 353, 1 August 1981, p. 38.

On Spectacles: "Considérations sur les lunettes", in *Les Lunettes*. Pierre Marly, editor. Paris: Atelier Hachette/Massin, 1980, pp. 5–9

Thoughts of Sorts: "Penser/Classer", *Le Genre humain*, no. 2, 1982, pp. 111–127.

VERSIONS

Slightly different versions of these English translations have appeared as follows: "Statement of Intent" and "81 Easy-Cook Recipes" in *Review of Contemporary Fiction*, XIII. no. 1 (1993), pp. 21–22 and 34–43; "Backtracking" in *Grand Street* 44 (1993), pp. 195–202.

"Statement of Intent" (as "Notes on What I'm Looking For"); "Notes on the Objects to Be Found on My Desk" (as "Notes Concerning the Objects that are on my Work-table"); "Brief Notes on the Art and Craft of Sorting Books" (as "Brief Notes on the Art and Manner of Arranging One's Books"); "Twelve Sidelong Glances"; "Backtracking" (as "The Scenes of a Stratagem"); "Reading" (as "Reading: A Socio-physiological Outline"); "On the Difficulty of Imagining the Good Life" (as "On the Difficulty of Imagining an Ideal City"); and "Thoughts of Sorts" (as "Think/Classify") have also been translated (I use the term loosely) by John Sturrock and published in Georges Perec, *Species of Spaces and Other Pieces*. London: Penguin, 1998.

OTHER REFERENCES

J. L. Borges, *Other Inquisitions*, trans. Ruth L. Simms. New York: Souvenir Press, 1973, p. 103.

Marcel Mauss, *Sociology and Psychology*, trans. Ben Brewster. London: Routledge, 1979, pp. 95–123. First published in French as Part IV of *Sociologie et anthropologie*. Paris: P.U.F., 1950.

The Pillow Book of Sei Shônagon, trans. Ivan Morris. New York: Columbia University Press, 1967.

THOUGHTS OF SORTS

has been set in Minion a type designed by Robert Slimbach in 1990. An offshoot of the designer's researches during the development of Adobe Garamond, Minion hybridized the characteristics of numerous Renaissance sources into a single calligraphic hand. Unlike many faces developed exclusively for digital typesetting, drawings for Minion were transferred to the computer early in the design phase, preserving much of the freshness of the original concept. Conceived with an eye toward overall harmony, its capitals, lower case, and numerals were carefully balanced to maintain a well-groomed "family" appearance – both between roman and italic and across the full range of weights. A decidedly contemporary face, Minion makes free use of the qualities Slimbach found most appealing in the types of the fifteenth and sixteenth centuries. Crisp drawing and a narrow set width make Minion an economical and easygoing book type, and even its name reflects its adaptable, affable, and almost self-effacing nature, referring as it does to a small size of type, a faithful or devoted servant, and a kind of peach.

DESIGN & COMPOSITION BY CARL W. SCARBROUGH